Preserving the Creation
Environmental Theology and Ethics

Contributors

Bernhard W. Anderson, is Professor Emeritus of Old Testament Theology at the Princeton Theological Seminary, Princeton, New Jersey, and Adjunct Professor of Old Testament at the Boston University Theological School in Boston, Massachusetts. Professor Anderson was co-director of the Drew-McCormick Archaeological Expedition to excavate the ancient biblical city of Schecem.

Andrew J. Christiansen, S.J., is Director of the Office of International Justice and Peace, United States Catholic Conference, Washington, D.C. A former Professor of theology at the University of Notre Dame, he writes extensively on social justice and the Catholic Church. Most recently, he is coauthor with George Lopez of *Morals and Might: Ethics and the Changing Use of Force in International Relations,* (Westview Press, expected Spring, 1994).

Richard J. Clifford, S.J., Professor of Old Testament at the Weston School of Theology, Cambridge, Massachusetts, is the author of numerous books and articles on the Old Testament.

Daniel M. Cowdin, Assistant Professor Moral Theology and Social Ethics at The Catholic University of America in Washington, D.C., was awarded the Richard J. Franke prize fellowship in the humanities at Yale University. His articles have appeared in the *Heythrop Journal* and the *Living Light*.

Gabriel Daly, O.S.A., a native of Dublin, Ireland, is Lecturer in Systematic and Historical Theology at Trinity College in Dublin. He is the author of *Asking the Father: A Study of the Prayer of Petition* (Michael Glazier, 1982) and *Creation and Redemption* (Michael Glazier, 1988).

Kevin Irwin, a priest of the archdiocese of New York, is Ordinary Professor of Liturgy and Sacramental Theology and Director of the Liturgical Studies program in the School of Religious Studies at The Catholic University of America in Washington, D.C. He also serves as advisor to the National Conference of Catholic Bishops' Committee on the Liturgy. His most recent work is *Context and Text: Method in Liturgical Theology* (Liturgical Press/Pueblo. 1994).

Elizabeth A. Johnson, C.S.J., is Professor of Theology at Fordham University in New York City and President Elect of the Catholic Theological Society of America. She is the author of *Consider Jesus: Waves of Renewal in Christology* (Crossroad, 1990) and *She Who Is: The Mystery of God in Feminist Theological Perspective* (Crossroad, 1992).

Edmund D. Pellegrino, M.D., is Acting Chief, Division of General Internal Medicine and the John Carroll Professor of Medicine and Medical Ethics at Georgetown University Medical Center. Dr. Pellegrino is also director of the Georgetown University Center for Clinical Bioethics, Washington, D.C.

Preserving the Creation
Environmental Theology and Ethics

EDITED BY
Kevin W. Irwin
and
Edmund D. Pellegrino

WITH THE EDITORIAL ASSISTANCE OF
Judith Lee Kissell

GEORGETOWN UNIVERSITY PRESS / WASHINGTON, D.C.

Georgetown University Press, Washington, D.C.   20007
Printed in the United States of America.
10 9 8 7 6 5 4 3 2 1   1994
THIS VOLUME IS PRINTED ON ACID-FREE OFFSET BOOK PAPER.

Library of Congress Cataloging-in-Publication Data

Preserving the creation : environmental theology and ethics / Kevin
    W. Irwin, Edmund D. Pellegrino, editors ; with the editorial
    assistance of Judith Lee Kissell.
        p.   cm.
    Collection of papers presented at the conference "Preserving the
    creation", held at Georgetown University, April 21-23, 1992.
    1. Human ecology--Religious aspects--Christianity--Congresses.
    2. Nature--Religious aspects--Christianity--Congresses.
    3. Creation--Congresses.   4. Human ecology--Moral and ethical
    aspects.   I. Irwin, Kevin W.   II. Pellegrino, Edmund D., 1920-
    BT695.5.P74   1994
    261.8'362--dc20
    ISBN 0-87840-549-6 (hard)   93-36684

Contents

KEVIN W. IRWIN

Introduction

In their recent insightful monograph, *Fullness of Faith: The Public Significance of Theology,* Michael and Kenneth Himes articulate the intrinsic relationship between systematic theology and ethics on a variety of topics and continually argue that such an articulation serves "public theology." They state that "public theology attempts to explicate the affinities between a religious tradition and a political opinion" and that "theology must be mediated by social ethics before it makes specific judgments about action."[1]

> What has sometimes been ignored is the distinctively theological underpinning for moral choices. For the church, one of the benefits of public theology is that it makes explicit the theological component of social ethics so that believers can understand and test the coherence of their religious beliefs with their public policy decisions.[2]

The papers collected in this volume can be characterized as an example of "public theology." The major aim of the "Preserving the Creation: Environmental Theology and Ethics," a symposium held at the Leavey Conference Center, Georgetown University, April 21-23, 1992, was to invite the composition and discussion of papers that would deepen and, we hoped, influence the ongoing contribution that theology can and must make to the contemporary discussion of concern for the environment. The conviction of the conference planners and the officers of the Bauman Foundation was that the Roman Catholic theological tradition has a particular and substantive contribution to make to a theology of creation and an ethical response to environmental concerns.

The delineation of scriptural, systematic, liturgical-sacramental, and ethical approaches seemed both obvious and reflective of the ways that Catholic theology may contribute substantively to this issue. In "The Bible and the Environment," Richard Clifford chose to avoid the temptation to collect and review texts "that express wonder before natural beauty or command human beings to care for the environment." Rather he chose to probe more fully and deeply "whether creation and care for the environment are truly important in the story of God and Israel, and if they are, to explain how." Among other things, Clifford argues, the bible contains the story of the human race as a society within culture, part of which is the natural environment. In the biblical cosmologies, human sin blights the earth while divine salvation restores people and their environment. Clifford argues that biblical assertions about the interrelatedness of humanity and the universe are profoundly complex and forbid a facile ethic of dominance or manipulation of creation. Biblical talk of creation, he asserts, is inevitably also eschatological speech. In Christ, community and humanity are located in the physical environment of the universe whose redemption is nothing short of cosmic.

In "Foundations in Systematics for Ecological Theology," Gabriel Daly argues that the contemporary crisis in the environment—"that planet earth is under siege, attacked and ravaged by its most intelligent animal species *homo sapiens*"—is physical in the sense that survival is clearly the issue. This ethical crisis, Daly claims, raises the question of whether we also have a theological crisis. Although classical Christian theology has claimed a theology of creation, the contemporary urgency about the environment suggests that the theology of creation has been seriously neglected and underdeveloped, especially in the West. In his paper, Daly shows how the theologies of creation and redemption can be related to one another in a way that avoids "the anthropocentrism and joyless sin-centeredness of much of the traditional approach." He concludes by offering insightful possibilities of the implications of a refurbished creation theology for other branches of theology. These include theology's relationship to solidarity with the poor, to ecumenism, and to ecofeminism.

In my own paper, "The Sacramentality of Creation and the Role of Creation in Liturgy and Sacraments," I have argued that the doctrine of sacramentality includes both how creation discloses and mediates an experience of the triune God and how a rich theology about the nature of God and God's act of creating (both past and present) is reflected in liturgy and sacramental practice throughout history and particularly in the contemporary reform of liturgy and sacraments. Liturgical celebration and sacramental practice presume and articulate—in word, ritual, symbol, and gesture—the theological value of the use of natural things (e.g., water) and things that are the product of human ingenuity (e.g., bread and wine). Their use can (and should) lead to the ethical consequences concomitant with liturgical celebration in terms of preserving creation. My argument supports and underscores two traditional theological premises: that the church's prayer reflects its belief (*lex orandi, lex credendi*) and that the liturgy's use of the sacramentality of creation reflects a sacramental vision of the Christian life that underscores the discoverability of God in human life. Because creation is regarded as a manifestation of God's presence and is a central medium for worshiping God, to emphasize the sacramentality of creation implies that worshipers will reverence creation and engage in efforts to preserve it.

Daniel Cowdin's modestly entitled paper, "Toward an Environmental Ethic," lays the groundwork for developing such an ethic through the Roman Catholic tradition. He is concerned to address why we ought to be constructing an environmental ethic, to reflect on what this ethic might entail and how it would interact with current moral theology, and to explore methodological options in its construction.[3] Cowdin argues that an environmental ethic, like other areas of social ethics, must involve knowledge of philosophy and applied sciences and is therefore necessarily a cross-disciplinary pursuit. He begins his argument by developing a "fundamental option" for nature at the deepest level, but at the same time, discusses a parallel articulation using natural law language. He then explores how this nature-centered option expands and enhances our sense of human dignity, especially in light of recent developments in ethical theory, and considers certain methodological issues on how to shape an environmental ethic. Here he is less concerned to delineate the specifics of the option as to indicate general directions and critique some approaches that seem vulnerable. He concludes by offering important ideas on linking nature with eschatology.

As expected, these papers and their responses offered much material for discussion and spirited debate at the conference. At the same time they disclosed a number of avenues for future development, including opening the discussions to third world theologians and third world experiences of hands-on care for the environment; probing more deeply the interrelatedness of systematic and liturgical-sacramental theology with social ethics in the Catholic experience of life and theology; and delving into the relationship of aesthetics to systematic theology and social ethics.

While a specific aim of the conference was to articulate a Roman Catholic contribution to the environment, the papers, responses, and discussions also reflected the breadth of ecumenical theology and concern for the environment. Further discussion across denominational lines is clearly necessary to enhance and nuance this contribution. Part of this conversation is already taking place in conjunction with the National Religious Partnership for the Environment. It is our hope that

the publication of these papers and responses will help foster an ongoing dialogue among theologians, ethicists, and public policymakers on
the issue of care for the environment.

NOTES

    1.   Michael Hines and Kenneth Hines, *Fullness of Faith: The Public Signif-
icance of Theology,* (Mahwah, NJ: Paulist Press, 1993), 22.

    2.   Ibid., 23.

    3.   Regrettably, Michael Himes's response to Kevin Irwin's paper could
not be included in this volume. See, however, his "Creation and an Environmental Ethic," in the *Fullness of Faith*, chapter 5.

Acknowledgments

Patricia Bauman initiated the idea for this conference. To her and to the staff of the Bauman Foundation, we owe profound and deep thanks for underwriting this meeting financially and for encouraging theological work that adds to public discourse on the environment. We are also deeply grateful to the meeting's co-sponsors: the Center for the Advanced Study of Ethics, Georgetown University, and the School of Religious Studies, the Catholic University of America. Judith Lee Kissell offered invaluable assistance in preparing this text for publication.

Richard J. Clifford, S.J.

The Bible and the Environment

The Christian Bible, that is, the Hebrew Bible and the New Testament, tells the story of God's people in the world. Its narratives, poetry, and laws reflect the interplay of people and physical environment. Given this biblical concreteness and contemporary sensitivity to our physical environment, one is tempted simply to collect texts that express wonder before natural beauty or command human beings to care for the environment. But simply collecting texts runs the risk of a new proof-texting—using biblical passages to support a contemporary position. The biblical theologian's task is rather to ask whether creation and care for the environment are truly important in the story of God and Israel, and if they are, to explain how. Many scholars of our era do not reckon creation and nature to be theologically significant in the Bible. We must therefore analyze carefully the problem of creation and environment in the Bible.

Several key texts and themes in the Bible lead to the conclusion that the human race and its natural habitat are indissolubly linked and that the race has a divinely given responsibility for the world. These conclusions run counter to modern interpretation of the Bible. They pose a challenge not only to biblical theology but to Christian theology as well for theology must be foundationally biblical as it explores today's questions and gives its answers in contemporary language.

Before examining biblical texts we must first note the considerable differences between contemporary Western common sense definitions of creation and environment and the viewpoints of the ancient Near East, the culture of the Bible. The differences are fairly obvious but failure to note them can lead to serious confusion about creation and nature in the Bible.

THREE QUALITIES OF ANCIENT COSMOGONIES

An ancient neareastern creation account, or cosmogony, differs in at least three ways from modern concepts of creation: the process of creation, the world that emerges, and the manner of reporting.[1]

1

The Process of Creation

Ancient neareasterners generally imagined creation on the model of human making or of natural activity. For example, the gods formed the world as an artisan works clay; they commanded it to exist as a king's word makes things happen; they built it as one builds a building or creation was imagined as a hillock bursting with life derived from the Nile as it receded from flood level. Creation was frequently pictured as a conflict of beings endowed with wills; the creator god vanquished inert or hostile forces, typically personified as a sea monster. Ancient texts did not make the modern distinction between "nature" and human beings and sometimes offered psychic and social explanations for nonhuman phenomena.

Modern writers, on the other hand, influenced by scientific and evolutionary thinking, understand creation as the impersonal interaction of physical forces extending over eons. They do not use human activity as a model for impersonal forces.

The Product or World that Emerges

To the ancients, a *peopled* universe emerged from the creation process. Though the texts are theocentric, that is, the gods create for their own ends, human society is nonetheless prominent and usually imagined concretely with a culture that includes kingship, tools, and a physical environment (marshes, rivers, animals). Moderns usually imagine creation issuing in the world of planets and stars. Human society and culture are not in their purview.

Manner of Reporting and Criteria of Truth

Ancients often reported creation as a drama whereas moderns write scientific reports. Each type of recording corresponds to a concept of creation—evolutionary, according to "impersonal" laws of nature, or dramatic, modeled on human or natural activity. To explain new data, scientists offer new hypotheses whereas ancient poets devised new stories or introduced variations on existing tales.

Modern readers sometimes find it difficult to take ancient creation stories seriously. Because we customarily use stories for entertainment or illustration, we can fail to appreciate narrative as a route to philosophical or theological truth. Where modern sensibility does take narrative seriously—in history—ancient creation narratives scandalize for their readers because the same event appears in several versions. For example, Sumerian literature had two cosmogonic systems,[2] and Akkadian literature preserves at least thirteen different "minor cosmogonies"[3] in addition to the epics *Enuma elish* and *Atrahasis*. Each Egyptian sanctuary had its own system.[4] Even the Bible contains different cosmogonies in Genesis, Proverbs, Job, Psalms, and Second Isaiah. Their aim is not scientific accuracy but the explanation or exploration of a present reality by describing its origins. These "stories of origins" come at their subjects from many angles.

Biblical scholars have not always recognized how integrally the human race fits within the physical world. One cause of their insensitivity is Reformation epistemology. The sixteenth-century recovery of the Bible, which founded modern biblical scholarship, put less value on knowledge gained from the senses (on the grounds that it was distorted by sin) than on knowledge gained from God's word addressed to human beings in history. It tended to devalue natural reason over scripturally revealed knowledge. History as a concept of biblical theology came to dwarf the concept of nature. The tendency was encouraged by post–World War I Protestant Neoorthodoxy which exalted Christian revelation over natural theology. Other philosophical and theological currents moved in the same direction: the "turn to the subject" in modern philosophy, the existentialist concern with individual authenticity, and the "anthropological" approach in recent Roman Catholic theology. One need not deny the validity of these approaches to concede that they can create a climate affecting one's ability to notice the role of nature and the environment in the Bible.

OLD TESTAMENT TEXTS AND THEMES

The Bible contains many texts and themes about human responsibility for the environment.[5] Of the many, this article can discuss only a few—and these only from the perspective of the human race and the environment. These include, in the Old Testament, Genesis 1–11, the role of land and environment in the formation of Israel and in the covenant blessings and curses, and Isaiah 40–66; and in the New Testament, Romans 8:18–30, Colossians 1:15–20, and John 1.

Genesis 1:1–2:3

Genesis 1–3 is without doubt the preeminent biblical source for Western imagery of creation. Its shaping took place during the traumatic sixth-century Babylonian Exile when the Priestly or P editors (so called because of their interest in chronology and rituals) revised the venerable national story (conventionally called J) for the needs of the exiles. Genesis 1:1–2:3 now prefaces the creation-flood story in Genesis 2:4–11:26 providing an interpretative lens through which exiles from the land of Israel, anxious about their future and their claim on ancestral land, could read Genesis and indeed the entire Pentateuch.

The parallel structure of the six days in Genesis 1 shows the relation of the human race to the environment.[6]

"Began": Chaos

1 Light (Day)/Darkness (Night) = 4 sun/moon
2 *raqia'* between waters   = 5 fish and birds from waters
3 a) dry land   = 6 a) animals
  b) vegetation   b) man: male/female
7 "finished" fulfills "began" of verse 1

The cosmogony has some affinities to Mesopotamian cosmogonies, for example, the taming of a boundless sea; but there are significant differences. That Genesis depicts the human in royal terms is suggested by the words "image" and "likeness" (found in Mesopotamian royal inscriptions) and by the verbs "rule" and "subdue."[7] In Mesopotamian cosmogonies human beings are invariably slaves, created to maintain the universe for the gods who are by vocation idle. When Mesopotamian accounts have a king, he is created separately from the human race to oversee its service of the gods. Genesis 1 portrays the man (who with the woman stands for the race *in nuce*) as a king, and the human task is far broader than temple maintenance. The God of Genesis does not need human servants as do the other gods; the human race consequently has a different relation to work and to the world.

The universe that arises in Genesis 1 is in a special sense a *system*, a network in which the elements of the world are hierarchized and assigned value. Ancient cosmogonies were systems, at least implicitly. Sometimes the system was articulated by describing the precreation period as the mirror image of the created world, for example, "a holy house . . . had not been made; a reed had not come forth, a tree had not been created."[8] More often the system was implied by the actual sequence of divine actions, for example, the gods plan, tame the sea or channel the cosmic waters, create the marshes to supply mud bricks and reeds for the temple, form the human race as slaves and animals as potential sacrifices, and bestow cultural implements such as work tools.

In comparison with Mesopotamian systems, however, Genesis 1 stands out for its complexity and coherence and in not being completely oriented to the care and feeding of *'Elohîm*, God. The parallel scheme has already shown the interconnections: days one through three correspond to days four through six and day seven (God's rest) is *extra-seriem* as a climax. Though penultimate in relation to the whole week, the man and woman on day six are the center of a web stretching backward and forward through all seven days. The fifth-day divine blessing of the birds and fishes (1:22) is repeated in expanded form over the human couple (1:28). The phrase for reproduction of each species, "plants yielding seed, and fruit trees bearing fruit in which is their seed, each according to its kind" (1:11, 21, 24) is trans-posed for the human race: "male and female [God] created them." Sex-uality, "male and female," is the human version of the reproductive capacity inherent in life forms, a means for sustaining the universe.[9] Further, the human race is linked to each of the three constituent tiers of the world by dominion over sea, heaven, and earth (1:26). The human race rules (*radâ*, 1:26) the animal life of each of the three domains, as the sun and moon govern (*mashal*) day and night. And only the human race by its climactic sixth day position (and by its free-dom to respond to the divine word) directly encounters God.[10]

In the Genesis system, the human race is the linchpin of a harmoni-ous universe, spanning it, uniting it, and bringing it before God. Because God is not needy, the system is designed less immediately to provide essential services for the divine world. God's actions do not make things for the divine world—marshes for the bricks and reeds for the temple, animals for its sacrifices, and human beings to build it—but things for the human race to play its role in the world. In the course of the week, the world is made fit for human habitation; darkness is made into night and enveloping waters into seas.

Another indication of a harmonious system is the reshaping rather than destruction of chaos. God puts it to a new use: darkness is made part of a restorative day and night sequence and the waters are rele-gated to the sea where they can no longer prevent life from arising. The reworking of chaos is especially clear in Psalm 104. Verses 5–18 describe the divine master of the waters enveloping the earth; the waters flee like panic-stricken warriors before God's rebuke (5–9) and become fertilizing rivers and rain (10–18). In verses 19–23, God demon-strates the same mastery over darkness.

Does the divine command to the human race in Genesis 1:26, 28 "to have dominion over" the fish, birds, cattle, and creeping things and "to fill the earth and subdue it"[11] give permission to the human race to manipulate and exploit the world? Taken out of their narrative context, the verbs used in this passage indeed seem to warrant an instrumental view of the nonhuman. But the narrative context shows that they do not. That human dominion is to be exercised in a royal way is implied by the phrase "image and likeness" and the verbs of ruling. In the ancient Near East, the king imaged or "re-presented" his divine patron in heaven by acting for the god and thus resembling this god in a dynamic rather than static way. The king promulgated laws establish-ing divine justice on earth, fought the god's battles, and oversaw the temple ceremonial for the god's benefit.

In Genesis 1, the human race exercises dominion over the three realms of sea, heaven, and earth by ruling the highest form of life in each. The best illustration of active dominion in Genesis is the just man Noah prior to the flood. According to the P narrative Noah brought two individuals (male and female) of every kind of animal into the ark to keep them alive with him (6:19). God's command to the first man to be fruitful and multiply, (1:28), that is, to continue in existence, evidently implied that the human race was to keep other forms of animal life in existence, to save them from destruction. Noah's saving the animals was certainly not an act of narrow self-interest, for at that time humans were not permitted to kill animals for meat (1:29–30). Not until after the flood was eating meat allowed as a concession to the inherent violence of the human species.

The phrase in verse 28 "subdue the earth" is also problematic for modern readers because the verb "subdue" is often used of forceful military domination. Syntactically the verb expands and completes the preceding phrase "fill the earth" rather than the following "have dominion over." The fish and birds had been told in verse 22 to "increase and multiply and fill the waters of the sea" but not to subdue it. The addition of the verb "subdue" in verse 28 suggests that the human race will encounter problems as it takes its habitat. The underlying idea seems to be the same as Genesis 10 and Deuteronomy 32:8–9: God gives to each people its own land. Each nation is to take its divinely apportioned land; Israel is given Canaan but must wrest it from its inhabitants. "Earth" is not then land in general but the particular land given to each nation. "Subdue" may be a proleptic reference to Israel's conquest of Canaan (Joshua 18:1 and Numbers 32:22, 29 use the same verb) which is then taken as typical for all nations.[12] The forcefulness implicit in the verb is associated with each nation's first-time seizure of their God-given land.

Thus, the opening chapter of the Bible shows us the human race exercising God's rule over the world. That rule is limited on the one side by the divinely articulated system of which human beings are a part and on the other by God in whose name the race exercises its rule.

A final note on the eschatology, or orientation to the future, hidden within Genesis 1. The text says nothing about the reality of human sin but declares seven times that creation is good. The statement is not an empirical deduction but a divine word that must prevail. The text presents the world *God* has made and thus the world that *will be*. That at least is how the author of Revelation interpreted the Bible's opening chapter; the last book of the New Testament ends with creation renewed (Revelation 21:1–22:5), chaos having been forever vanquished (Revelation 19:11–20:15).[13] Other biblical texts will refer to the original order and harmony of the new age, for example, Isaiah 11:1–9; 65:25; Ezekiel 47:1–12, and Revelation 21:1–22:5.

Genesis 2:4–11:26

Genesis 2–3 (Adam and Eve) is often assumed to be a story complete in itself and called "the second of two accounts of creation," but this view cannot be defended on literary or comparative grounds. Rather Genesis 2–3 begins a single story that ends only in 11:26. Both the dramatic structure of Chapters 2–11 and similarly-plotted extrabiblical stories, such as the Mesopotamian epic *Atrahasis* (seventeenth-century B.C.), strongly suggest that the chapters form one story. Genesis 2–11 is not strictly speaking "a second creation story" but the main story, introduced by Genesis 1. It provides an interpretive lens to the reader of the following chapters.

Chapters 2–11, like Genesis 1, also show that the human race is part of a system, only here the length and sophistication of the story illustrate the historical, cultural, and ecological dimensions of the system. The story belongs to the genre of creation-flood epic that explores human culture through narrative.[14] The genre has an ideal plot: the gods create the world and the human race; human disturbance of the gods provokes them to send an annihilating flood; after the flood the gods restore their creation but adjust the design of the human race so that its population will never again get out of hand. *Atrahasis* is a particularly relevant example of the genre because its theme of overpopulation—the expansion of the human race beyond the capacity of the land—also shows up in an altered way in Genesis.[15]

Relation of land to human population is only one of many "cultural" issues in Genesis 2–11. Others are sexuality and marriage (Chapters 2–3), evil and its intergenerational effects (Chapters 3–4), nomadism, animal husbandry, music, metallurgy, worship, and cities (Chapter 4), and different races, languages, and lands (Chapters 10–11). The texts explore these elements of culture by describing their origin; the first instance of a phenomenon reveals its essence when the impress of the divine hand was still fresh. A special concern of the epic is the limits of culture imposed by divine and human folly and by death.

The creation-flood genre shows how historical and relational biblical anthropocentrism truly is. In Genesis 2–11 the human race (in typical figures) acts within a history of cause and effect, is thoroughly rooted in its environment, and is subject to a just and powerful God. The man (*'adam*) is created from earth (*'adamâ*, in 2:7; the wordplay underlines the close link) and becomes a living being when God breathes into his nostrils the breath of life.[16] In Genesis 2:8, the man is created to be a gardener whose work is required for the earth to bloom (2:6). The LORD God brings all animals and birds to the man so he can name them: "and whatever the man called every living creature, that was its name" (2:19). Naming cannot be reduced to possessing power over another since the man in 2:23 names his wife whom God gives him expressly as a "compatible helper" in contrast to the subordinate and "incompatible" animals previously brought to him. From the context naming connotes appropriate authority, affinity, and care.[17]

The primordial bond between the human beings and the earth appears also in the series of alienations caused by the couple's sin and its effect on the earth. Eve's childbearing will take place in pain, and Adam's gardening will be done by the sweat of his face upon a resistant soil; "cursed is the ground because of you." Several generations after Adam and Eve the earth is again affected by human disobedience.

> Now the earth was corrupt (šaḥat) in God's sight, and the earth was filled with violence. And God looked on the earth and it was corrupt; for all flesh had corrupted its ways upon the earth. And God said to Noah, I have determined to make an end of all flesh, for the earth is filled with violence because of them; I am about to destroy them along with the earth (Genesis 6:11–13).

"Earth" occurs six times and the verb "to corrupt" is used both of human beings and of nature. Earth shares in the frightful consequences of human sin.

After the flood, God restores the system; the human race is again its responsible center. To Noah and his household, God reaffirms the original command of Genesis 1:28: "Be fruitful and multiply, and fill the earth" (9:1). In comparable post-flood restorations, the gods put limits on human population (childbirth demons, celibate women, mortality). But in Genesis God does not alter the original blessing; the original design was perfect.[18] But there is one change: "The fear and dread of you shall rest on every animal of the earth", as well as on birds, creeping things and fish (9:2). All animals are given to the human race for food, with one proviso: the blood of the slain animal must be poured on the ground, for the blood is the life (9:4–6). The life shared by human and animals is not under human authority. As if in compensation for the new vulnerability of the animals, God makes one covenant with both humans and animals as witness to the bond between all sentient beings:

> I am now establishing my covenant with you and your descendants after you, and with every living creature that is with you, the birds, the cattle, and every beast of the earth with you, all who came out of the ark . . . that never again shall all flesh be destroyed by the waters of a flood (Genesis 9:9–11).

The rainbow is the covenant's sin, signaling that all future rainstorms will end short of deluge proportions.

The concession to human perversity represented by the permission to shed blood in Genesis 9 serves to underscore the original harmony of the world God created. The prophets allude to the original harmony of the universe before human sin and express the hope of its return. Hosea 2:18, 21–22 (Hebrews 2:20, 23–24) states:

> I will make for you a covenant on that day with the wild animals, the birds of the air, and the creeping things of the ground, and bow, sword, and war I will abolish from the land; and I will make you lie down in safety. . . . On that day I will answer, says the LORD, I will answer the heavens and they shall answer the earth; and the earth shall answer the grain, the wine, and the oil.

Isaiah 11:1–0 sees a future restoration through the davidic king, clothed in righteousness and faithfulness, when "the wolf shall lie with the lamb, the leopard shall lie down with the kid." Isaiah 65 sees Zion being created anew—new buildings, extraordinary human longevity and harmony between animals and human beings: "The wolf and the lamb shall feed together, the lion shall eat straw like the ox" (Isaiah 65:25). The ending of the Gospel of Mark names as signs accompanying the apostolic preaching speaking in new tongues, picking up snakes in the hands, not being harmed by deadly potions (Mark 16:17), which evoke the Hebrew Bible's "peaceable kingdom" statements. According to Revelation 21:1–22:5, all sinners will be expelled from the heavenly Jerusalem (21:8) which will then become the source of the water of life (cf. Genesis 2:10–14) and of all varieties of fruit. Biblical metaphors should not of course be prosaized into doctrine:

> No one with a grain of sense believes that . . . Isaiah 11 is intended literally, as though the digestive system of a carnivore were going to be transformed into a herbivore.[19]

The biblical texts contrast our experience of decay and violence in the universe with the order and peace of God's kingdom.

Christian interpretation has tended to neglect the cultural and ecological dimension of Genesis 2–11 because theological tradition has focused on Chapters 2–3, the story of Adam and Eve, as Claus Westermann has pointed out.[20] Paul's New Adam christology (most completely set forth in Romans 5:12–21 and 1 Corinthians 15:21–23, 45–49) may have unwittingly been one cause of the dislocation. The contrast of Adam's disobedience and Christ's obedience directs Christian attention to Chapters 2–3 at the expense of Chapters 4–11, implying that sin primarily affects individuals (Adam and Eve) and that redemption redresses only individual sins. Such a reading underrates sin as destructive of society and the environment and redemption as restoration of the divinely ordered system. Paul himself was not so narrow. Romans 8:18–30 uses the New Adam christology (cf. "image" in 8:29) to affirm that both nature and the human race are damaged by sin and groan in pain as they wait for deliverance.

Genesis 2–11, chiefly through narrative and genealogy, gives a sophisticated portrait of the human race situating them as creatures in the world created by God. The chapters are indeed anthropocentric in the sense that the human race lives within a history shaped by God's word and on an earth that shares the same destiny.

Before leaving Genesis 1–11 we ought to notice their unique perspective. In contrast to the ethnocentrism of many extrabiblical cosmogonies, these chapters are entirely about the nations, the *goyîm*. The distinction between the nations and Israel, which is extremely important in the Hebrew Bible, is introduced only when Israel explicitly comes on stage in the person of Abraham (beginning in Genesis 11:27). In the Bible, Israel addresses the nations precisely as the exception, as the contrast society. The following passages about Israel are paradigmatic for the nations.

The Formation of Israel

When Israel enters on the biblical stage in a preliminary way with Abraham and fully with the leading out of Israel in Exodus, the inherent orientation of people to land is dramatically seen. Abraham and Sarah are landless and childless (the very themes highlighted in Genesis 1). Their story and the story of their descendants Isaac, Jacob, and Joseph revolve around land and progeny. The twin themes play an even more crucial role in the Book of Exodus. The Book begins with Pharaoh's attempt to frustrate the Genesis blessing of progeny and land by destroying the Hebrew children (Exodus 1:10, 15–22) and keeping the people from their land (Exodus 1:10). The remarkable feature of Exodus, as Norbert Lohfink has pointed out, is that the LORD enters Egypt the domain of Pharaoh (portrayed in godlike terms) to bring Israel from there to his own land.[21] The redemption is intensely land-bound: the people were servants to Pharaoh *in Egypt* and now are servants to the LORD *in Canaan*. The LORD's land is described in mythic terms: "a land of milk and honey" (e.g., Exodus 3:8, 17; 13:5; Leviticus 20:24 [Hebrews]; Numbers 13:27; Deuteronomy 6:3; 11:9; Joshua 5:6; Jeremiah 11:5; Ezekiel 20:6, 15), so that the journey leads to a place of natural abundance as well as political freedom.

The festival commemorating the liberation from Egypt is the spring ritual of Passover, combining the rites of the lamb and unleavened bread (*maṣṣôt*). The two rituals were originally separate, one a rite of herders to propitiate the gods when the tribe moved from the well-watered winter pastures to the arid summer ones, and the other a rite of farmers, a kind of spring cleaning of the previous year's leaven. All scholars agree they were made into a commemoration of the historical exodus from Egypt,[22] but not all give due weight to the inescapable fact that the rites remain *agricultural* feasts, commemorating the abundance of the LORD's land.

The intrinsic bond of Israel to the land as a political and agricultural reality is shown in the covenant, a key biblical institution. The covenant is a legal agreement, sworn before the gods, expressing the fundamental relationship between the LORD and Israel. The book of Exodus records how God rescued the Hebrews from Pharaoh's oppressive Egypt and brought them to God's own land of Canaan. On the way to Canaan at Sinai, God and people defined their new relationship by the covenant, embodying it in the Ten Commandments (Exodus 19–20) and Covenant Code (Exodus 21–23) and ritually celebrating it (Exodus 24). The book of Deuteronomy develops the theology of the covenant, especially its demand for absolute loyalty. The covenant promised blessings for loyalty and curses for disloyalty. The curses and blessings were concerned with the land and were couched largely in military and agricultural terms: invasion or protection of the land; abundance or famine. One vivid formulation of covenant blessing is Deuteronomy 28:11–12.

> The LORD will make you abound in prosperity, in the fruit of your womb, in the fruit of your livestock, and in the fruit of your ground that he swore to your ancestors to give to you. The LORD will open for you his abundant storehouse, the heavens, to give the rain of your land in its season and to bless all your work.

The eighth-century prophets Amos and Hosea were the first to preach that the covenant had come to an end. They announced the curses but raised the hope that after the judgment the blessings of the covenant would come. Hosea announced a time when the LORD would take back "my grain in its time, and my wine in its season; and I will take away my wool and my flax" (Hosea 2:9; Hebrews 2:11). In Hosea's post-punishment restoration God will

> make for you a covenant on that day with the wild animals, the birds of the air, and the creeping things of the ground; and bow,

sword, and war I will abolish from the land; and I will make you lie down in safety (Hosea 2:18; Hebrews 2:20).

In Amos 4:4–11 God uses five natural afflictions—famine, drought, blight and mildew, plague, and a Sodom-and-Gomorrah-like "over-turning"—to punish and warn Israel. But the postjudgment restoration of Israel (Amos 9:11–15) means both political and environmental sha-lom: the rebuilding of the davidic kingship, the defeat of enemies, and abundant fertility: "The mountains shall drip sweet wine, and all the hills shall flow with it."[23]

Isaiah 40–66

Another prophetic book, Second Isaiah develops two relevant themes: salvation as the healing of nature, and salvation as the purification and restoration of the holy city of Zion. Students of the book of Isaiah increasingly recognize that its sixty-six chapters are thematically uni-fied; themes raised by Isaiah of Jerusalem in the eighth century are developed by Second and Third Isaiah for their sixth-century audi-ence.[24]

Salvation as the healing of nature: Chapters 40–55 urge the sixth-century exiles in Babylon to embark on a new exodus to their home-land Palestine; just as their ancestors had become Israel in the fullest sense by leaving Egypt and entering God's land Canaan, so the exiles are again to become Israel by leaving Babylon for Zion. To describe this restorative work of God, the prophet uses language of creation and language of redemption complementarily: God leads the people through the wilderness in a new exodus and a new land-taking: God destroys the "chaos" of the wilderness, reshaping it so the people can march through it to Zion.

The prophet's juxtaposition of cosmogonic and historic language and perspective to describe saving events has a good biblical prece-dent; in the venerable hymn in Exodus 15, the LORD, the storm god, defeats Pharaoh's troops at the sea. Isaiah 43:16–21 is an excellent example of the complementary use of creation and redemption lan-guage.[25]

[16]*Thus says the LORD,*
   the one who makes a way in the Sea,
      a path in the Mighty Waters,
   [17]*the one who musters chariot and horse,*
      all the mighty army;

> they lie prostrate, no more to rise,
>> they are extinguished, quenched like a wick:
> ¹⁸Recall no more the former things,
>> the ancient events bring no longer to mind.
> ¹⁹I am now doing something new,
>> now it springs forth, do you not recognize it?
> I am making a way in the wilderness,
>> paths in the desert.
> ²⁰The wild beasts will honor me,
>> jackals and ostriches.
> For I have placed waters in the wilderness,
>> rivers in the desert.
> to give drink to my chosen people,
> ²¹the people whom I have formed for myself,
>> to narrate my praiseworthy deeds.

The LORD is the conqueror of Sea (cosmogonic language) and Pharaoh's troops (historical or redemption language). Verses 18–21 replace the recital of the traditional crossing of the sea with a new recital: the crossing of the wilderness. The new event repeats the old act: a way in the Sea parallels a way in the wilderness; a path in the Mighty Waters parallels paths in the desert. This time it is not the sea but the impassable desert that keeps the people from their land. The problem the desert poses to the people is not its lifelessness per se but its interposing itself between Israel and the land; it blocks the people from entering their land. The highway over which the LORD will lead the people will be so safe for humans that the exotic desert animals will join in worship and there will be abundant water for "the people you have formed for yourself."

The healing of the environment as part of redemption is not confined to Chapters 40–55. Isaiah 11:1–9 responds to the threat of the Assyrian king by envisioning (in 6–9) the time of a future davidic king:

> The wolf shall live with the lamb,
>> the leopard shall lie down with the kid.
> the calf and lion and the fatling together,
>> and a little child shall lead them.
> The cow and the bear shall graze,
>> their young shall lie down together,
>> and the lion shall eat straw like the ox.

> *The nursing child shall play over the hold of the asp,*
>> *and the weaned child shall put its hand on the adder's den.*
> *They will not hurt or destroy on all my holy mountain;*
>> *for the earth will be full of the knowledge of the* LORD *as the*
>> *waters cover the sea.*

Isaiah 35 is another text that parallels the healing of the desert and the healing of restored humanity.[26]

> *The wilderness and the dry land shall be glad,*
>> *the desert shall rejoice and blossom.*
> [5]*Then the eyes of the blind shall be opened,*
>> *and the ears of the deaf unstopped;*
> [6]*then the lame shall leap like a deer,*
>> *and the tongue of the speechless sing for joy.*
> [7]*For waters shall break forth in the wilderness,*
>> *and streams in the desert (35:1, 5–7).*

The people of Israel are so much a part of their environment that their healing means healing for nature too.

Zion as the site of God's judgment and new creation: In the Bible, Israel is oriented to Zion, the LORD's dwelling. So close is the bond between city and people that the city suffers in God's purifying judgment (e.g., 1:21–28; 28:1–22; 29:1–8) and like the people, comes through it renewed and recreated (1:21–28; 45:14–25; 49:14–26; 54; 60–62; 65; 66). Chapter 65 explicitly calls the restoration after judgment a new creation.

> *For I am about to create new heavens*
>> *and a new earth;*
> *the former things shall not be remembered*
>> *or come to mind. . . .*
> *I will rejoice in Jerusalem*
>> *and delight in my people;*
> *No more shall the sound of weeping be heard in it,*
>> *or the cry of distress. . . .*
> *No more shall there be in it*
>> *an infant that lives but a few days,*
>>> *or an old person who does not live out a lifetime. . . .*

²⁸ The wolf and the lamb shall feed together,
the lion shall eat straw like the ox;
but the serpent—its food shall be dust!
They shall not hurt or destroy
on all my holy mountain,
says the LORD *(Isaiah 65:17, 19, 20, 28).*

The hope expressed in the chapter is not otherworldly like certain popular conceptions of heaven. Belief in resurrection and an afterlife in the Bible come long after this text. This hope is down to earth in good biblical fashion: long life with good health, children, wealth, a secure household, honor from the community. The environment here is both natural and made. The text expects that God will reward the righteous and vindicate their works (65:13–17). God creates a new city, transforming the faithful people *including* their buildings and habitat. The timetable of the new creation however, is in God's hands: "I am the LORD; in its time I will accomplish it quickly" (Isaiah 62:22).

Excursus on eschatology and apocalyptic: The mention of God's transformation of the people and their deeds is an appropriate time to discuss briefly a topic often joined to creation—eschatology. Eschatology, the doctrine of the future God intends for Israel and the human race, is a persistent theme in the Bible because God's words and activities are enduring and purposeful. For example, God's promise to Abraham and Sarah is truly fulfilled in their lifetime, and because God's word is never exhausted, is fulfilled again in the exodus and land taking, and yet again in Christian faith modeled on Abraham (Romans 4). Biblical hopes are realistic and concrete, directed toward a renewed version of the present on the basis of God's fidelity and power.

The way we understand eschatology bears directly on human responsibility for the environment. For example, if God utterly annihilates the present world to make a new one, why should one care for this world? In such a scenario how we act, our motivation, might be important but not what we do, for the "what" will be annihilated. If on the other hand, God creates our world anew, destroying what is sinful and bringing to perfection what is good, then what we do is exceptionally important—it will be incorporated into God's new creation for which the Bible hopes. In the second case God would not create *ex nihilo* as in the first creation but (partially at least) from the work that human beings have done.

One strand of biblical tradition seems to deny any value to the present age. Apocalyptic eschatology emphasizes the utter evil and vanity of the present age and eagerly awaits its passing away. A difficulty in discussing apocalyptic is the lack of scholarly consensus regarding its definition and historical development. To bring some clarity to scholarly terminological confusion Paul Hanson defines apocalyptic eschatology as

> neither a genre, nor a socio-religious movement, nor a system of thought, but rather a religious perspective, a way of viewing divine plans in relation to mundane realities. . . . The difference [from prophetic eschatology] involves the degree to which divine plans and acts are interpreted as being effected within the structures of mundane reality and through the agency of human persons.[27]

The apocalypses of Daniel (Chapters 7, 8, 10–12), the little apocalypse of Mark 13 and its parallels, and the Book of Revelation are examples of apocalyptic eschatology. Fully developed apocalyptic eschatology discloses a reality that transcends temporally and spatially the present world in order to show the ultimate triumph of God especially when human agents of change are nowhere in evidence. Apocalyptic eschatology indeed seems to deny any value to the world, hence implying that any care for it is useless. One can nonetheless ask whether such apocalyptic eschatology intends ultimately to denigrate the present world and teach that the future world will be utterly discontinuous with the present or to reshape the imaginations of powerless people to include an active God.

Proverbs 3:13–26 and 8

The Book of Proverbs gives memorable expression to everyday experience. It presumes that order is built into the universe and that people can discover it and live their lives accordingly. Proverbs 10–31 is a collection of proverbs, mostly "two-liners," in which one line plays off against the first. Chapters 1–3 contain essaylike poems that are more sustained probings of life in the world. Proverbs 3:13–26 is one such essay that places at its exact center an important teaching on creation.[28]

[19]*The LORD by wisdom founded the earth,*
Established the heavens by understanding.
[20]*By his knowledge the deeps burst apart;*
The clouds dropped down dew.

Formal analysis shows that verses 13–26 form a single poem: six bicola precede the creation passage in verses 19–20 and six bicola follow, thus making the two verses on creation central; the seven substantives in the poem for "wisdom" occur only in the centerpiece (19–20), in the first colon of the first section (13) and in the first colon of the second section (21*b*). There is also logical coherence: in verses 13–18 the person who finds wisdom is declared blessed (* '*šr* 13*a*, 18*b*) in having life, wealth, honor, favor, peace, but the explanation is given only in verses 19–20: The LORD built the world "by wisdom"; those who live "by wisdom" will enjoy the fruits of this world. The second set of six bicola (21–26) exhorts the hearer to seek those same gifts—life, favor, blessing on one's "walking," removal of fear. People therefore must keep shrewdness and foresight, synonyms for wisdom, before their eyes (21, cf. Deuteronomy 6:8). God has so constructed the world that people can be touched by a divine quality within it.

The long poem of Proverbs 8 makes the same point but is more explicit that God implanted Wisdom in the world to invite people to life. Wisdom, personified as an attractive woman, rejoices both in her intimate association with The LORD in heaven and with human beings on earth. She was there when the physical world was created ("When he established the heavens I was there . . . when he marked out the foundations of the earth, I was beside him like a master worker," (Proverbs 8:27, 30). Related intimately to the LORD of creation she offers an analogous intimacy ("daily" in verse 34) to those who wait at her door and listen to her teaching. Wisdom is within the world speaking God's appeal. The world is not mute or morally neutral but is able to address every seeker after life.[29]

The Book of Job

The Book of Job differs sharply from Proverbs on human beings' ability to know the world and be confident in its design and order. The drama opens in heaven: unbeknownst to Job and his friends, God, at the suggestion of Satan (an official in God's employ, not the devil of later times) decides to put the righteous Job to the test. The opening ironic dissonance between human knowledge and divine intent is maintained throughout the book. Provoked by his suffering and his three friends, Job complains bitterly in lengthy speeches of God's treatment of him and the universe, demanding that God respond to him.

God's answer to Job in the climactic chapters 38–41 is a description of the created world in two parallel speeches; and the large-scale parallelism evidently produce resonances for the ancient hearer. The logic of the speeches is better shown by Norman Habel's outline than by extensive citation.

A. Introductory 38:1
   formula with report
   of theophany event
B. Thematic challenge: 38:2–3
   i. Theme A
       "Who is this
       who clouds my
       design . . .?"
   ii. Summons
       "Gird your loins"
C. Elaboration of theme
   i. in the physical
       world 38:4–38
   ii. in the animal
       kingdom 38:39–39:3
D. Challenge to Legal
   Adversary 40:1–2
E. Answer of Job 40:3–5

A1. Introductory 40:6
    formula with report
    of theophany event
B1. Thematic challenge: 40:7–14
    i. Theme B
        "Would you
        impugn my
        justice?"
    ii. Summons
        "Gird your loins"
C1. Elaboration of theme
    i. with Behemoth 40:15–24

    ii. with Leviathan 40:25–
        41:26: [40:1–34E]

E1. Answer of Job 42:1–6

God's lengthy description of the created world contains at least two surprises when the description is compared with ancient neareastern cosmogonies—there is no mention of the human race, and chaos (symbolized by the primordial land creature Behemoth and the primordial sea creature Leviathan) is *not* vanquished but only put on God's leash.[30] The divine speech affirms design and justice in the world (in the sense of being able to "judge" or uphold the right); but human beings are not the goal or purpose of creation, and their knowledge is decidedly limited (Chapter 28). Moshe Greenberg concludes from these chapters:

> How different this survey of creation is from that of Genesis 1 or the hymn to nature of Psalm 104. Here man is incidental—mainly an impotent foil to God. In Genesis 1 (and its echo, Psalm 8) teleology pervades a process of creation whose goal and crown is man. All is directed to his benefit; the earth and its creatures are his to rule. . . . Job, representing mankind, stands outside the picture, displaced from its center to a remote periphery.[31]

Job as a person is nonetheless important in the book. God directs a long speech exclusively to him; and judging by the many allusions in God's speech to Job's speeches, pays him the supreme compliment of listening to his every word. But even Job, legendary for his wisdom and justice, cannot fathom the world God has created. The book forces the reader to reinterpret biblical anthropocentrism within an irreducible theocentrism.

THE NEW TESTAMENT TEXTS

For New Testament writers during the last half of the first century of the Common Era, and beginning of the second, the Hebrew Bible was "the scriptures." The early Christians accepted it, lived by it and within its pages found validation for the career of Jesus Christ and support for his teaching. To Christians, Jesus ushered in the New Age depicted in the scriptures—a time of creation harmony, covenant blessing, political and environmental shalom—in a word the Kingdom of God. The New Testament's view of the environment is essentially that of the Old Testament: human beings are an integral component of the good world created by God. Damaged by sinful human behavior, the world in its human and nonhuman aspects is to be redeemed, re-created by Christ. And human beings, irreducibly corporal, are to be saved, healed in "body and soul."

Relatively few New Testament passages deal explicitly with creation or the environment, but the basic New Testament proclamation—Jesus Christ has been raised from the dead—is a major statement about human beings' relation to the world. The resurrection is interpreted as a new creation because Christ, the representative human being, has defeated death, the enemy of the race and hence of the world. Christ's act is like the defeat of darkness and the waters (the primordial human enemy) in the first creation. His resurrection as representative human being, raises up the world as a system because the human race is an integral part of that system.[32]

A clear statement of Christ's act as new creation is the hymn in Colossians 1:15–20.

> [15] *He is the image of the invisible God,*
>   the first born of all creation.
> [16] *For in him were created all things in heaven and on earth,*
>   *the visible and the invisible,*
>   *whether thrones or dominions or principalities or powers;*
>   *all things were created through him and for him.*
> [18] *He is the head of the body, the church.*
>   He is the beginning, the firstborn from the dead.

Creation and reconciliation are described in parallel stanzas, verses 15–17 and verses 18–20, each containing fifty-five words.[33] Parallelism is a standard biblical way of developing ideas. In creation Christ was the image (*eikōn*, cf. Genesis 1:27–28) of the invisible God, the firstborn of creation in the sense that the created world is modeled on him, oriented to him, subordinate to him, cohering in him. The phraseology is largely derived from Genesis 1 and the personification of wisdom in such texts as Proverbs 3:19–20 and 8:1–36. In Genesis, darkness and chaos were overcome so that the human community can be formed. Proverbs urges people to shun the path of death for the path of life.

The second part, verses 18–20, applies Christ's role in creation analogously to his work in the church. The two sections, creation and new creation, are united by impressive formal parallels: "he is" is repeated in chiastic order (*hos estin . . . hotos estin* in verses 15, 17; *hotos estin . . . hos estin* in verse 18); "firstborn," underlined above, occurs in both sections; "whether . . . or . . ." occurs in verse 16–20. The virtual identity of verses 16*d* and 20*a*, *ta panta di autou kai eis auton ektistai* and *kai di autou apokallaxai ta panta eis auton*, makes creating (*ektistai*) parallel to reconciling (*apokallaxai*). The basic statement of the text is that new creation begins in Christ just as first creation did. Instead of the word "creation" (which occurs three times in part one), part two uses three different phrases, "firstborn of the dead," "reconcile," and "make peace."

Especially relevant for the topic of environment, the text states that the world is involved: the phrase "all things" is repeated six times and *ℓ* "heaven and earth" (16, 20) is a Hebrew idiom for the world. Christ's resurrection raises up the whole world, not just the human race. Ephesians 1:3–14, with its remarkable triadic structure of Father, Son, and Spirit, also uses the phrase "all things" and "heaven and earth" for the saving act of Christ:

> In all wisdom and insight, he has made known to us the mystery of his will in accord with his favor that he set for in him as a plan for the fullness of times, to sum up all things in Christ, in heaven and on earth.

Though the whole universe is created anew, creation begins at a particular point—the chosen people. New life radiates from the risen Christ upon those closest to him. New Testament writings express the idea of life in a variety of ways, for example, "remaining in Christ," obeying Christ, the bread of life and the wine in the Gospel of John; but occasionally they employ the word creation for the emergence of the new people as in 2 Corinthians 5:17:

> So whoever is in Christ is a new creation; the old things have passed away; behold new things have come. And all this is from

God, who has reconciled us to himself through Christ and given us this ministry of reconciliation.

The text alludes to Isaiah 43:18–21 which also describes the new act of God in the language of both creation and redemption. Galatians 6:15 uses new creation similarly.

The hymn in John (originally perhaps verses 1–5, 10–11, 14) resembles Colossians 1:15–20 in blending Genesis 1 and wisdom texts to describe the work of Christ.

> ^{1}*In the beginning was the Word,*
> *and the Word was with God,*
> *and the Word was God.*
> ^{2}*He was in the beginning with God.*
> ^{3}*All things came to be through him,*
> *and without him nothing came to be.*
> *What came to be ^{4}through him was life,*
> *and this life was the light of the human race;*
> ^{5}*the light shines in the darkness,*
> *and the darkness has not overcome it.*
> ^{10}*He was in the world,*
> *and the world came to be through him,*
> *but the world did not know him.*
> ^{11}*He came to what was his own,*
> *but his own people did not accept him.*
> ^{14}*And the Word became flesh*
> *and made his dwelling among us,*
> *and we saw his glory,*
> *the glory as of the Father's only Son,*
> *full of grace and of truth.*[34]

The hymn employs metaphors already developed in John's gospel: Jesus is the true light illuminating humankind and Wisdom addressing words of life to his followers. John raises the light and divine word of creation in Genesis 1 to the ethical plane. The darkness and disorder resulting from unbelief are overcome by God's word and light in Christ. Christ is legitimated by the scriptures as the Word and the Wisdom who brings the world to completion.

Romans 8:18–30 describes cosmic redemption another way. In good biblical fashion, Paul places nature and human beings in parallel as they respond to divine acts.[35] Nature here waits for deliverance as eagerly as any human being, for it too has been damaged by the sins of the human race:

> For creation awaits with eager expectation the revelation of the children of God; for creation was made subject to futility, not of its own accord but because of the one who subjected it, in hope that creation itself would be set from slavery to corruption and share in the glorious freedom of the children of God (Genesis 3:17–19; 6:11–13).

James Dunn sees this as a reference to the Adam narratives and takes "futility" in the sense of a role for which a thing was not designed:

> As man's futility is his assumption that he is an independent creator, the failure to realize that he is but a creature, so the futility of creation is its being seen solely in relation to man (as man's to use or abuse for himself) or as autonomous, an entity in its own right, to be deified in turn (Nature, the Universe), instead of as God's creation to be ordered by God.[36]

Paul uses the New Adam comparison again in 8:29:

> For those he foreknew he also predestined to be conformed to the image [Genesis 1:28] of his Son, so that he might be the firstborn among many brothers.

The Synoptic gospels are less grandly reflective than John on Christ as the creator, but even here Christ's salvation means the healing of human beings and their environment as is clear in the healing miracles. The focus, however, seems more person-centered in the gospels than in the Old Testament. In Matthew 11:5–6, Jesus fulfills Isaiah 61:1 and 35:5–6 (the blind receive their sight, the lame walk, the lepers are cleansed, the deaf hear, the dead are raised, and poor have the good news preached to them), but there is no reference to the healing of the wilderness.

Jesus in his parables frequently uses analogies from nature. The parables presume God is revealed in nature in such a way as to illuminate the kingdom: "Hear this!" A sower went out to sow his seed:

> To what shall we compare the kingdom of God, or what parable can we use for it? It is like a mustard seed that, when it is sown in

the ground, is the smallest of the seeds on the earth. But once it is sown, it springs up and becomes the largest of plants and puts forth large branches, so that the birds of the sky can dwell in its shade (Mark 4:30–32).

Against anxiety and unnecessary striving, Jesus advises, "Look at the birds of the sky. . . . Learn from the way the wild flowers grow" (Matthew 6:26, 27). Jesus' language is not merely "poetic," a concrete and memorable way of putting a truth. His metaphors reveal something profound about the structure of being: the underlying unity between the world of everyday experience and the reign of God. One is reminded of the message in Proverbs where Wisdom is in "heaven and earth" and makes her appeal to the sincere seeker.

In the New Testament, God sums up in Christ all previous modes of self-manifestation—hand, face, word, wisdom, spirit. Jesus is not more "spiritual" than previous modes of divine outreach but more embodied, more enfleshed. As man (in the inclusive sense) he can represent Israel and the human race as previous modes of divine presence could never have.

CONCLUSION

The anthropocentrism of the Bible is relative, not absolute. It is bounded on the one side by a pervasive theocentrism and, on the other, by the created world of which the human race is a constituent, albeit the crowning, part. The human race rules as God's representative or image over the world as a system, not over the world as discrete manipulable elements. Human beings are the responsible center of the world, in the root sense of ability to respond. Their dominion maintains the will of the creator regarding the world. The Book of Job adds its own radical qualification to biblical anthropocentrism. Chapters 38–41 insist that God created the world for his own inscrutable purpose and not for the human race; human beings will never fathom the divine purpose of the world (Chapter 28). But paradoxically human beings are important in the book and in the created world.

Though not identified with nature, God is the power behind the fertility and infertility of the natural world. Depending on the quality of its relation to God, Israel experiences the world as nurturing or destructive. God is particularly present in the land of Israel; the people live from its riches and define themselves as a nation by its soil. The formulation of the covenant blessings and curses presumes Israel's rootedness in the land—security or invasion, fertility or blight.

Biblical cosmogonies connect society and its environment. Human sin blights the earth and divine salvation restores the people and their environment. In visions of the future, the Bible sometimes does not distinguish sharply between the human and nonhuman world. For example in Isaiah 65 and its New Testament parallel in Revelation 21:1–22:5 re-created Zion has its buildings restored, its faithful poor vindicated, and nature appears again in its original harmony.

The New Testament interprets the resurrection of Jesus as a new creation; Christ's rising from the dead defeats the primordial enemy of human community in a manner analogous to the first creation in which chaos was defeated and the human race began to live. The analogy was easy for ancient near eastern people to draw, for they understood creation primarily as the emergence of a people. New creation is not however, identical to first creation, for first creation creates out of chaos or nothingness whereas new creation creates out of sinful or ambiguous human history.

NOTES

1. R. Clifford, "The Hebrew Scriptures and the Theology of Creation, *Theological Studies* 46(3): 507–23.

2. J. van Dijk. Le motif cosmique dans la pensée sumérienne. *Acta orientalia.* 28(1–2): 1–59.

3. See J. Bottéro and S. N. Kramer, *Lorsque les dieux faisaient l'homme: Mythologie mésopotamienne*, Bibliothèque des histoires (Paris: Galatianslimard. 1989); and the earlier and less complete A. Heidel, *The Babylonian Genesis*. 2d. ed. (Chicago: University of Chicago, 1951), Chapter 2.

4. James P. Allen, *Genesis in Egypt: The Philosophy of Ancient Egyptian Creation Accounts.* Yale Egyptological Studies 2 (New Haven: Yale), 1988.

5. An excellent orientation to the topic with bibliography is the collection of essays in B. W. Anderson, ed., *Creation in the Old Testament.* Issues in Religion and Theology 6 (Philadelphia: Fortress, 1984). See especially the essay by Anderson, "Creation and Ecology," 152–71.

6. I am indebted to B. W. Anderson, "A Stylistic Study of the Priestly Creation Story." In *Canon and Authority*, ed. G. W. Coats and B. O. Long (Philadelphia: Fortress, 1977), 148–62.

7. Phyllis Bird, "Male and female he created them: Genesis 1:27b in the context of the priestly account of creation." *Harvard Theological Review* 74(2): 129–59. Especially 140–44. In discussing ancient accounts of creation, I will occasionally use "man," generally in an inclusive sense, to preserve concreteness. All translations of the Old Testament are my own. All translations of the New Testament are from the Revised New Testament of the New American Bible.

8. Line 1 of the Chaldean cosmogony, Heidel, *Babylonian Genesis*, 62. Genesis 2:4–6 and Proverbs 8:22–26 similarly mirror the created order. The elaborate precreation tableau of Sumer and Dilmun was interpreted by Pascal Attinger in 1984 as a social system in Enki and Ninhursaga (*Zeitschrift für Assyriologie* 74(1): 33–34.

9. Bird, "Male and female," 146–47.

10. Sirach 16:24–18:14 (or at least 16:24–17:24), which is based on Genesis 1–3, affirms the common link to the earth of both the human (17:1–4) and nonhuman (16:26–30) worlds. At the same time, it contrasts the regularity and unfailing obedience of nature with the freedom and responsibility of the human race.

11. The exaltation of the human race is even more evident in Psalm 8: "You have made him [human beings] ruler over the work of your hands,/ you have put all things under his feet" (7). But Psalm 8 maintains a strong tension between God's sovereignty ("How powerful is your name in all the earth") and lowly humans' awesome responsibility.

12. N. Lohfink, *The Priestly Document and the Limits of Growth: Great Themes from the Old Testament* (Edinburgh: T. &. T. Clark, 1982), 167–82; and R. J. Clifford. "Genesis 1–3: Permission to exploit nature?" *The Bible Today* 26(3): 133–37.

13. Claus Westermann. *Beginning and End in the Bible.* Facet Books Biblical Series 31 (Philadelphia: Fortress, 1972).

14. David Damrosch proposes the genre label in *The narrative covenant: Transformations of Genre in the Growth of the Biblical Tradition* (San Francisco: Harper, 1987), chapters 1–3. The genre includes Mesopotamian compositions such as the Sumerian Flood Story (Thorkild Jacobsen's *Eridu Genesis*), *The Rulers of Lagash*, Tablet XI of Gilgamesh, and *Atrahasis*.

15. See Anne Kilmer, "The Mesopotamian Concept of Overpopulation and Its Solution as Reflected in Mythology." *Orientalia* 41(2): 160–77. Tikva Frymer-Kensky, *Biblical archaeologist* 40(4): 147–55, recently summarized in W. L. Moran, "Some Considerations of Form and Interpretation in *Atra-Hasis*." In *Language, Literature and History: Philological and Historical Studies Presented to Erica Reine*, American Oriental Series Monograph 67, ed. F. Rochberg-Halton (Winona Lake: Eisenbrauns, 1987), 245–55. For the viewpoint that the problem is human fault, see R. Oden. *Zeitschrift für die alttestamentliche Wissenschaft* 93(2): 197–216.

16. Biblical anthropology does not presuppose a spirit-body dualism; the human person is an enfleshed spirit. The occasional contrast in the Bible between "flesh" and "spirit" is not internal (body-soul) but external; "flesh" is the human person relying on personal strength, whereas "spirit" is God's power.

17. Indispensable on Chapters 2–3 is Phyllis Trible, "A love story gone awry" in *God and the Rhetoric of Sexuality* (Philadelphia: Fortress, 1978), 72–143.

18. A point made especially by W. L. Moran, "Atrahasis: The Babylonian Story of the Flood." *Biblica* 40(1): 51–61.

19. C. F. D. Moule, *Man and Nature in the New Testament.* Facet Books. Biblical Series 17 (Philadelphia: Fortress, 1967), 11.

20. Claus Westumann, *Creation* (Philadelphia: Fortress, 1974), chapter 1.

21. N. Lohfink, *Option for the Poor: The Basic Principles of Liberation Theology in the Light of the Bible* (Berkeley: BIBAL, 1987), chapter 2. The importance of the land of Canaan in defining the exodus is correctly emphasized by J. Levenson, "Liberation Theology and the Exodus," *Midstream* 35(1): 30–46.

22. R. de Vaux, *Ancient Israel* (New York: McGraw-Hill, 1964), 484–93.

23. Most scholars deny these verses to Amos though on not very convincing grounds. For a recent spirited defence, see S. Paul, *Amos*, Hermeneia (Milwaukee: Fortress, 1991).

24. For a summary of recent scholarship, see E. W. Conrad. "Reading Isaiah." *Overtures in Biblical Theology* (Minneapolis: Fortress, 1991).

25. Reading *ntybt* with 1QIs[a]. *Naharôt* has been attracted from 20*d*.

26. F. M. Cross, "The Redemption of Nature," *Princeton Seminary Bulletin* 10(2): 94–104.

27. "Apocalyptic," in *Interpreter's Dictionary of the Bible*, Supplementary Volume (Nashville: Abingdon, 1976), 29–31.

28. W. Zimmerli takes verses 13–26 as a unit in *Sprüche, Prediger* ATD 16,1 (Göttingen: Vandenhoeck and Ruprecht, 1962), 21–22, as does P. Doll. *Menschenschöpfung und Weltschöpfung*, Stuttgarter Bibelstudien 117 (Katholisches Bibelwerk, 1985), 49. R. B. Y. Scott sees three different pieces, verses 13–18, 19–20, and 21–26, in *Proverbs Ecclesiastes*, Anchor Bible 18. (Garden City: Doubleday, 1965), 45–48; W. McKane sees verses 13–20 as a poem without verses 21–26, in *Proverbs: A New Approach*, Old Testament Library (Philadelphia: Westminster, 1970), 289–90, 294–99; R. Murphy takes verses 13–24 as an instruction introduced by a hymn (13–18) in *Wisdom literature*, Forms of Old Testament Literature (Grand Rapids: Wm. B. Eerdmans, 1981), 57–58.

29. For development of the similar idea of righteousness as the divinely implanted order in the universe, see H. H. Schmid, "Creation, righteousness, and salvation: 'Creation theology' as the broad vision of natural theology," B. Anderson, ed. *Creation in the Old Testament*, 102–17.

30. In the analysis of Job's speech, I follow mainly Norman Habel, *The Book of Job*, Old Testament Library. (Philadelphia: Westminster, 1985).

31. "Job" in R. Alter and F. Kermode, eds., *The Literary Guide to the Bible*. (Cambridge: Harvard University Press, 1987), 298.

32. An admirable attempt to link the resurrection of Christ to the renewal of creation is R. C. Van Leeuwen, "Christ's resurrection and the Christian's vindication," in *The Environment and the Christian: What Does the New Testament Say about the Environment?* (Grand Rapids: Baker, 1991), 57–71.

33. That is, when the poorly attested phrase "through him" of verse 20 is excised.

34. *New American Bible*. Revised.

35. Psalms 114 and 148 and Daniel 3:26–90 (Greek text) are among innumerable biblical examples of this practice, as is Psalm 98:7–8:
Let the sea and what fills it resound, / the world and those who dwell there. / Let the rivers clap their hands, / the mountains shout with them for joy.

36. *Romans 1–8*. Word Commentary 38 (Dallas: Word, 1988), 470.

The Sacredness of the Earth

BERNHARD W. ANDERSON

Richard Clifford has offered us a rich treatment of those scriptures that provide a firm foundation for the Christian theologian to address our pressing ecological concerns. While his coverage embraces the whole Bible from the Old Testament to the New he has given us a particularly in-depth treatment of the early chapters of Genesis and the message of the book of Isaiah.

GENERAL HERMENEUTICAL CONSIDERATIONS

In the course of discussion, Clifford has laid down three basic hermeneutical principles.

1. He warns us against prooftexting and the appeal to isolated texts in support of our ecological responsibility. The creation story of Genesis 1 must be read contextually, that is, in the context of the primeval history of Genesis 1–11. Prooftexting has resulted in taking texts out of their scriptural context as in the case of the passage in Genesis 1:26–28 concerning human dominion over the creation. Misuse of the latter text drew the fire of Lynn White, Jr., in his famous 1967 essay, "The Historical Roots of Our Ecological Crisis," in which he endeavored to trace the philosophical and theological origins of the environmental crisis to the Judeo-Christian doctrine of creation.

2. Biblical texts are appropriately read in the larger context of the culture of the ancient Near East though due attention must be given to their distinctive witness. This larger contextual reading helps us to understand, for instance, the royal role of human being implied in the *imago Dei*, as well as the structural pattern of creation to chaos (flood) to new beginning, which the biblical primeval history shares with other documents of the ancient Near East.

3. Biblical texts deal with philosophical or theological truth in a narrative or, as I would say, mythopoeic manner; that is, their poetic imagination contrasts with the discursive, abstract language of science. Whether on analysis these two kinds of knowing yield two kinds of truth is a matter for discussion. It is clear, however, that this narrative mythopoeic approach is socially oriented, for it assumes the position of storytellers in their society. As Clifford points out, the aim is to explain and explore "present reality," not to achieve "scientific accuracy" by trying to stand outside the scheme of things and view the world or nature objectively.

SPECIFIC ISSUES FOR DISCUSSION

Rather than provide a running commentary on this paper, which is both stimulating and enlightening, let me lift up some specific issues that deserve further discussion.

First—and this comment is on the paper as a whole—on biblical grounds Clifford rightly challenges the sharp dichotomy between nature and human culture or, we might say, between creation and history, which has been the dominant assumption of modern thought. The history of nature is intertwined with the history of human society. Consequently, as the Bible says in divers manners, the natural environment is affected by the tragedy of human history, even as the whole realm of nature will ultimately share in the redemption of the children of God as Paul states so magnificently in Romans 8:18–23.

This approach is salutary; it makes us realize that concern for the environment is not just our concern, belatedly, but fundamentally God's concern as expressed in the acts of divine judgment and restoration to which scripture bears witness. Care for the environment belongs essentially to God's creative and redeeming work that includes human beings universally and the nonhuman creation as well.

It is, however, no weakening of this statement and just as important, I believe, to turn to those "texts of rapture," to use Clifford's elegant phrase, which awaken in us awareness that the universe is sacred. Planet Earth belongs to God, not to human beings. As the psalmist exclaims:

> *The earth is the* LORD's, *and all that is in it,*
> *the world, and those who live in it,*
> *For God has founded it on the seas,*
> *and established it upon the rivers (Psalm 24:1).*

And the universe in which this planet is located is suffused with the glory of God: *"The heavens are telling the glory of God, and the firmament proclaims his handiwork."* (Psalm 19:1).

How different this view is from the modern notion that the universe is a mathematical system, like a machine or computer, that we can study or exploit for human purposes! Without falling into an idolatrous worship of the powers of nature we need to recover some of the spirituality of the Native Americans with their sense of the earth's sacredness and the wonder of the heavens. In the Bible, creation language is fundamentally doxological.

Second, Clifford helps us to understand that *'adam* (humankind), whose creation occurs at the climax of the biblical drama, is portrayed in royal terms. That is the meaning of the statement that *'adam* is made in the image of God, or in parallel formulation, in God's likeness. This view is supported by ancient near-eastern texts that describe the monarch as the "image of God" who represents the divine sovereign in mundane affairs. In the perspective of inner-biblical exegesis this view is also corroborated by Psalm 8 in which the royal role of the human being (*'enosh / / ben 'adam*) is emphasized. The psalmist's question, "What is man that you are mindful of him?" is answered with the exclamation that humanity is elevated toward the cosmic level of God's heavenly council (the *'ĕlōhîm* or angels).

This earthling, so tiny and ephemeral in contrast to the moon and stars, God has "crowned with honor and glory," has made "to rule" (*mashal*) over God's creative works, and has subjected "everything" like booty beneath the feet of a king. The language of "image" is dynamic, not static, as Clifford observes. Human being, consisting of male and female, is called to participate in God's administration, to be a co-regent with God and thus to manifest God's concern for creatures and uphold the *shalom* (well-being, harmony) of God's creation. I may add that the command, "be fruitful and multiply," which unrestrained and unrestricted leads to overpopulation, must be exercised with prudent control if human beings are to fulfill the rest of the divine commission: to exercise wise dominion over the earth.

What needs to be added to these reflections if we are to consider the whole picture is that human beings are closely related to, and even dependent, on nonhuman creatures. This point is made beautifully in Psalm 104 (especially verses 27–30), which is a liturgical parallel to the Genesis creation story. In Genesis 1, human affinity to the animal world is suggested by the coincidence of the creation of land animals (beasts and domestic cattle) and of *'adam* on the same day, the sixth. Furthermore, human beings, like the fish, birds, and land animals, are characterized as *nefesh hayya*, "living being." It is noteworthy that the appearance of living being or biological life occurs on the fifth day of the creation drama and is marked by a literary pause in which God expresses approval of this aspect of creation and gives a special blessing to the beings associated with the waters: the marine creatures that swim through the waters and the birds that fly over them. This is a narrative way of emphasizing "reverence for life," to use Albert Schweitzer's phrase—reverence for both animal and human life.

The scene portrayed in Genesis 1 is one of peace between animals and human beings like the famous painting of "the peaceable kingdom." Even when the order of creation is modified at the time of the Flood, and human beings are allowed to eat animal flesh, the Noachic covenant enjoins reverence for life, especially for the supreme form of living being, 'adam, who is made in the image of God (Gen 9:1–7). Thus, there is "an eschatology hidden within Genesis 1," as Clifford nicely puts it, for this picture corresponds to the envisioned consummation of all things when human and nonhuman creatures will take their proper place in the order that God has ordained, human beings acting as God's responsible agents to help maintain the harmony and equilibrium of creation.

As Clifford indicates, the Flood story fills out the picture portrayed in Genesis 1. The Noachic covenant, based on reverence for life is an ecological covenant; it is made with "all flesh," that is, human and nonhuman creatures, and with the earth itself. Noah is portrayed as one who fulfills the God-given commission to take care of the animals and birds (the fish are not mentioned because they are not threatened by water). Indeed the narrator describes the various species of *nefesh hayya* as coming to Noah (Gen 7:9) in the time of catastrophe; thereby, they become, along with human beings, members of the remnant with which God makes a new beginning.

Finally, Clifford's treatment of the paradise story in Genesis 2–3 provides an opportunity for us to move through the various prophetic passages, especially Isaiah 40–66, into the New Testament. He joins with Claus Westermann in criticizing the church's use of the Adam-Christ typology to foster an individualistic gospel of salvation, for concentrating on Genesis 2–3 "at the expense of Genesis 4–11." I, too, deplore a "person-centered" gospel that lacks the full dimension of social and ecological concern. Whether this weakness inheres in the New Testament or belongs to a particular reading of the New Testament is a matter for discussion. In my view, much depends on how the early Christian community, and especially Paul, Christianity's first major theologian, appropriated and transformed the apocalyptic eschatology inherited from the Old Testament (e.g., Zechariah) and Judaism (cf. the Qumran community).

Here a major issue is the difference between prophetic eschatology, as found in the writings of the classical prophets, and the apocalyptic eschatology that reaches its full-blown development in Zechariah 14, the apocalypse of Daniel, and the writings of the Pseudoepigrapha (especially 1 Enoch). "The Dawn of Apocalyptic," as Paul Hanson puts it, occurred when the heavenly vision, which prophets were commissioned to announce to society, could no longer be translated into mundane affairs owing to the changed sociological situation of oppressive evil and victimization by world powers.

Hanson's thought is a suggestive way of describing the difference between prophetic and apocalyptic eschatology. In any case, apocalyptic characteristically views this present world as under the dominion of evil, often symbolized as the mythical powers of chaos: sea, mighty waters, the floods, Rahab, Leviathan. Here we find a more radical view of evil—one that perceives suffering not just as deserved punishment for sin but also as victimization by sinister forces at work in human history. The consequence of this perception is that apocalyptic writers tend to make a sharp contrast between "this present age" and "the age to come."

In this connection, I have trouble with Clifford's statement about "the intent of apocalyptic eschatology." It is not ". . . to denigrate the present world and teach that the future world will be utterly discontinuous with the present or rather to reshape the imaginations of powerless people to include an active God." Apocalyptic thought may function to encourage people to stand firm against hopeless odds, but it is doubtfully a challenge to sense "the residual health" of society and bring about social change. An apocalyptic passage like Isaiah 24:1–20 portrays a radical change in human history that will come through a divine catastrophe, comparable to the Great Flood, when God will devastate the earth.

> *The earth is defiled by its people,*
> *they have disobeyed the laws,*
> *violated the statutes,*
> *and broken the everlasting covenant (Isaiah 24:5).*

This text refers to the Noachic covenant with its requirement of reverence for life.

The New Testament, however, breaks with the "two ages" view of apocalyptic with its sharp historical discontinuity: the present age under the power of evil, the age to come as the time when God's kingdom will rule on earth as in heaven. In various ways, the New Testament witnesses affirm that already the leaven of God's kingdom of God is at work in this world (Luke 13:20); already people are able to taste the powers of the age to come (Heb 6:5); already God's victory in Christ is liberating people not only from the power of sin but from all powers that hold God's creation, both human and nonhuman, in bondage (Rom 8:35–39); already the new creation has dawned even before the old has passed away (2 Cor 5:17). No longer are the two ages like two circles that touch tangentially; rather, the circles have begun to overlap. The implications of this Christian transformation of the apocalyptic vision are tremendous and far-reaching, especially in our time of ecological crisis. Even in this present evil age, when violence corrupts the earth (think of the preface to the Flood Story!) and when the earth itself is being violated, people are invited into a community that stands on the frontier of the kingdom of God and to act as responsible agents in God's redemptive purpose that spans all human history and includes the whole realm of nature.

I have pursued these matters in several collections of which *From Creation to New Creation*, is forthcoming from Minneapolis: Augsbury-Fortress Press.

Gabriel Daly, O.S.A.

Foundations in Systematics for Ecological Theology

Very few people can be unaware that planet Earth is under siege, attacked and ravaged by its most intelligent animal species, *homo sapiens*. It should be said straightaway that no one is deliberately setting out to destroy our planet; however, our way of life is taking place at the planet's expense, and that expense has now reached crisis proportions. We have to change the course of our lives if our planet is to survive as a habitat for living creatures, nonhuman as well as human. Our planet is sick and can be saved from death only by radical action on its behalf by the species that has caused the sickness. That action will make painful demands, especially on the life-styles of those who live in the developed world. We have here a physical crisis, namely, that of survival. We have here an ethical crisis, namely, that of recognizing where we have gone wrong and what we now have to do—not for our sakes only but for generations yet unborn.

Have we also a theological crisis? The answer is yes, of course, we have a theological crisis. From a Christian standpoint, you cannot have a physical and ethical crisis that is not theological.

I draw attention to the crisis that is upon us although the topic of this paper is not this ecological crisis but the theological task it has uncovered. I shall not dwell on the various ways in which we are poisoning our planet. Others can do that far better than I. My task is less dramatic and less immediately urgent than chronicling our human mistreatment of our planet. I wish to consider the theological situation that is revealed almost as a by-product of the ecological crisis. We have recently become aware that the Christian theology of creation has been seriously neglected and underdeveloped, especially in the West. This situation has long been in need of theological attention, irrespective of the contemporary ecological crisis. The crisis, however, adds a note of urgency to the task.

In the first of three sections, I shall make some methodological observations, after which I shall consider how certain theological attitudes have contributed to a serious neglect of the theology of creation. That we have been excessively anthropocentric in our traditional theological attitudes seems undeniable; but I shall nevertheless argue strongly against an equally excessive antihumanism, which would, I believe, be self-defeating.

In the second part of the paper, I will examine how the theologies of creation and redemption may be related to one another in a way that avoids the anthropocentrism and joyless sin-centeredness of the traditional approach. We need to take scientific cosmology, including evolutionary theory, with seriousness and integrate it into our theology of creation and salvation.

The third section of the paper considers some implications of a refurbished creation theology for other branches of theology.

METHODOLOGICAL OBSERVATIONS

Many theologians working in the area of creation opt for one or other form of the method of mutually critical correlation. I am most at home with David Tracy's understanding of the theological task as "self-conscious interpretation" through which an attempt is made "to establish mutually critical correlations between an interpretation of the Christian tradition and an interpretation of the contemporary situation."[1]

In respect to creation theology, I suggest that three correlations are particularly relevant:

1. the correlation between contemporary ecological consciousness and biblical texts that bear on the theology of creation;
2. the correlation between contemporary ecological consciousness and various strands of Christian tradition, some of which may themselves be interpreted in terms of conflict, for example, the Augustinian and the Cappadocian; and
3. the correlation between contemporary ecological consciousness and scientific and philosophical developments of the last three centuries, for example, Cartesian epistemology and Newtonian mechanics, which have had an influence on Christian theology.

In addition to these diachronic correlations between present and past, synchronic correlations occur between different schools of contemporary Christian theology. Two seem to call for special attention:

1. the correlation between contemporary ecological consciousness and the liberation movements on behalf of the poor and oppressed; and
2. the correlation between contemporary ecological consciousness and the feminist critique of patriarchy which, when com-

bined with the ecological critique of contemporary attitudes to the environment, produces the school of thought commonly described as ecofeminism.

I have one further methodological observation to make. I believe that human imagination has a particularly powerful role to play in the area of creation and ecology. Consequently, at various points in my paper I shall advance some images derived from nature that I think grip not only the speculative mind but also the emotions and the affections. I shall call them "icons," because they can be used contemplatively or liturgically and because, in view of Paul Ricoeur's dictum that the image as symbol gives rise to thought, they can provide entry points into theological discourse. I see them as performing a role analogous to that performed by story in narrative theology. Indeed most of them imply a story.

As an example of what I mean let me advance my first icon: planet Earth as seen from space.

We have all seen that delicately tinted sphere set jewel-like against a black background. The astronauts, American and Russian, described it with awe and profound emotion. They found it more moving than the black space on all sides with its suggestion of worlds at the far ends of the universe. This sphere was home as seen by voyagers in a way that no mere earth-bound travelers had ever seen home. For most of them the experience was religious. Even those who did not speak explicitly of God spoke of an experience that can only be categorized as mystical. Edgar Mitchell seems to have spoken for most of them when he wrote

> Suddenly from behind the rim of the moon, in long, slow-motion moments of immense majesty, there emerges a sparkling blue and white jewel, a light, delicate sky-blue sphere laced with slowly swirling veils of white, rising gradually like a small pearl in a thick sea of black mystery. It takes more than a moment to fully realize that this is Earth . . . home.[2]

The astronauts saw its beauty first, then its fragility, then went on to reflect with profound emotion: this Earth is home. Our icon has the power to combine the aesthetic and the affective. Even a photograph can suggest to a lively imagination something of the power of the original experience. The image can be seen at two levels. On the most immediately available level, it is a literal picture of the planet we live on. On a symbolic level it portrays a world infinitely vulnerable to the depredations of the only creatures who are capable of appreciating its beauty and thinking of it as "home." Conversion to the task of doing all we can to save it begins in the imagination that is capable of "seeing" its invisible ozone layer, the blanket of gases that regulate its heat unless interfered with by predatory and self-indulgent humans, and its vesture of forests harboring innumerable threatened species and contributing to the life-enhancing features of the atmosphere.

James Lovelock calls it "Gaia"; his theory postulates the existence of earth not simply as a habitat for diverse living creatures but as itself a living creature regulating its own existence in response to various external and internal forces. "Gaia as the largest manifestation of life differs from other living organisms of Earth in the way that you or I differ from our population of living cells."[3] This daring and inspiring instance of holistic thinking helps fire the imagination and sets us thinking with aesthetic sensitivity, affection, and ethical determination about our planet as the work of God's hands. Lovelock puts forward his theory as a purely scientific one and has finds himself up against the forces of conservative biology with their built-in resistance to teleology and their endemic reductionism. Even if there are significant scientific objections to Lovelock's Gaia hypothesis, it still retains its symbolic truth.

Gaia and other nature-derived icons can help focus mind and heart on other imaginatively effective images of God's creation. As symbols they give rise to thought, and at that point we must again attend to hermeneutical questions. It is relatively easy to interpret our response to a nature-derived icon as a significant human experience. As Christians however, we have to correlate this experience with our interpretation of classical sacred texts, especially the Bible. My approach here is purely methodological; biblical scholars are better qualified than I to analyze those scriptures that refer to God's dealings with nature. Here I am concerned merely to note the hermeneutical problem that faces ecologically sensitive readers. The problem is similar to, if less intense than, that faced by any feminist who wishes to remain Jewish or Christian: how are we to treat canonical texts that offend against our most basic convictions?[4]

It can hardly be denied that certain biblical texts appear to see human beings as dominators and exploiters of the world. One has only to recall Genesis 1:28: ". . . fill the earth and subdue it," or Psalm 8:5: "You have given him dominion over the works of your hands." The problem is how to read such texts today. Several stratagems are possible. The text may allow for interpretations not envisaged by the author. (In poststructuralism this approach is not merely allowed but actively prescribed.) Or the text may be consciously read in a way that relativizes its cultural context so that it no longer makes a religious or moral claim on the reader. Or it may be read as witness to a situation lacking the religious and moral sensibility that a later age has made possible.

The biblical writers cannot be justly accused of contributing directly to our late twentieth-century anxieties about the future of the planet or of offending against our canons of ecological responsibility. It would be hermeneutically naive to expect the biblical authors to share our anxiety and guilt about the way we treat our world.[5] They cannot be held responsible for later interpretations of their words. After all, biblical texts have been invoked down the ages in support of all kinds of nefarious deeds. We may, however, have to school ourselves to read the Bible appropriately—to notice, for example, that its anthropocentric texts may be redressed in our imaginations by other texts, such as Psalm 104, the covenant with Noah, and the great fanfare of divine celebration of nature in the book of Job.

A similar situation arises with regard to patristic and other theological texts. Eastern Orthodox theologians regularly accuse Western Christian theology, Catholic and Protestant, of traditionally separating creation from redemption in a manner that is detrimental to a proper understanding and evaluation of creation. I shall return to this matter shortly; here, I wish to make a methodological observation about it. When, for example, the Orthodox theologian Paul Gregorios pits the theology of Gregory of Nyssa against that of Augustine, he makes a point that Western theology needs to hear in spite of its slightly triumphalistic tone.[6] Augustine did indeed give a direction to Western theology that is in serious need of adjustment if we are to construct a satisfactory theology of creation. Yet we cannot simply turn to Gregory of Nyssa or to other patristic theologians and expect them to speak convincingly to us in our post-Enlightenment world without considerable hermeneutical adaptation. What we can do is recognize that the patristic theologians who advanced a theology favorable to creation were unhappily obscured in Western theology and may be ripe for retrieval and further development. Patristic theology, whether Eastern or Western, will have to stand in mutually critical correlation with contemporary culture. It cannot simply stand in judgment over that culture. There has to be a hermeneutics of suspicion and retrieval: patristic fundamentalism is no more acceptable than biblical fundamentalism.

This hermeneutical observation leads me to a consideration of how certain directions taken in Western theology centuries ago diverted attention away from creation and nature. I single out the preoccupation with (1) divine transcendence, immutability, and impassibility; and (2) history as a framework for soteriology.

Transcendence

The term "transcendence" as applied to God has several possible references of which the ontological is the controlling instance: God is distinct in terms of being (*esse*) from all that is not God. The problem, of course, is how to affirm divine otherness without importing a note of distance. The metaphor of transcendence is, after all, a spatial one. God is being itself. All other beings are contingent, that is, being does not belong to them as a necessary predicate. This "aseity" of God, when coupled with other attributes denoting ontological perfection, such as impassibility, immutability, and omnipotence, sets up the concept of God in terms of God's *difference* from all that is not God. The difference is not of degree but of kind. It acts as a chasm preventing the affirmation of ontological continuity between God and the cosmos.

Not even the doctrine of the analogy of being can temper the force of the emphasis laid on the "differentness" and distinctness of God from creation. It underpins a solidly apophatic theology, which affirms that what we can know about God is infinitely outweighed by what we do not know, and it allows the time- and space-bound mind to think of transcendent reality. Yet because it is an epistemological rather than an ontological stratagem it does little to redress the emphasis placed by traditional scholastic theology on divine transcendence.

Aquinas says plainly that any relationship between God and creatures can exist only in creatures, never in God who remains unaffected by the divine work. Thus, the God of classical theism is the product of a one-sided development of the divine otherness. This relentless emphasis on divine transcendence tends to depict God as a monarch, a "cosmic moralist," someone "wholly lacking in receptiveness and responsiveness."[7] Such a God is a candidate for radical review in our age by process thinkers, feminists, and ecologically sensitive theologians. In a matter as problematic as God's relationship with, and action in, the world, perhaps the most satisfactory course is to work with a plurality of models in the knowledge that each has its possibilities and its limitations.

Some theologians (e.g., Moltmann, Kasper, and Boff) make extensive use of trinitarian theology in an effort to give the theology of God a new direction and impact. If I were convinced of the validity of their approach, I would discuss their arguments at this point. Unfortunately I am not convinced by Moltmann's "social trinity." To be frank, I am chary of any attempt to project on God sociopolitical convictions born of, for example, our dislike of patriarchy. Nor am I convinced by Walter Kasper's suggestion that a vacillating age needs a strong statement of trinitarian belief as a healthy alternative to the depredations of the Enlightenment.[8]

History as Framework for Salvation

In some respects, the Protestant turn to history as the field for divine revelation and salvation was the consequence of a preoccupation with divine transcendence and a deep suspicion of incarnational and sacramental attitudes to nature. Catharina Halkes makes the interesting remark:

> In contrast with Roman Catholic theology, which saw in nature and in the earthly reality references to God's immanence, and which preserved and respected the earthly, material reality in its sacraments, Reformed theology always trembled before nature and symbols of nature, as before a dangerous fascination which could adopt a demonic shape. The results of the fall go so deep that nature, by definition, is fallen nature.[9]

Only in history could the sovereign Word of God speak to sinful human beings. This approach was facilitated by the effects of the scientific revolution in the seventeenth century, after which the natural sciences entered on a course that took them further away from the arts and humanities, including theology. Theologians were happy to hand nature over to the scientists, who in turn were happy to deal with it in a way that had no need of God as a hypothesis. Protestant theologians were relieved to be rid of a possible source of conflict with scientists, but it has since become clear that they bought their peace at a heavy price. They turned to history, including critical study of the Bible, believing that they could discern in Israel a people who were not interested in nature or cosmos but only in history. As Adelbert Schloz puts it:

> Israel's God was not regarded chiefly as the Creator but as the Saviour. Israel understood its election as the obligation to separate not only from other peoples but also from their adoration of natural forces and localities, of sexual generation of life. This led to the demythologization of the idols.[10]

Nineteenth-century liberal Protestantism tended with Ritschl to regard nature as a hostile force set over against human beings who must achieve their specifically human destiny by conquering it. Thus, Wilhelm Hermann could write that "we can no longer hope to find God by seeking him in nature. God is hidden from us in nature. . . . It is only out of life in history that God can come to meet us."[11] This dogmatic assurance of where God can and cannot be found is part of the hubris of nineteenth-century liberal theology, though it has to be said that the Barthian nemesis was not brought to bear on this particular piece of liberal teaching.

This history-oriented view of theology influenced and in turn was influenced by Old Testament criticism. Gerhard von Rad and his school argued from the undoubted *historical* priority of Exodus over Genesis to the much more disputable *theological* priority of salvation over creation, which greatly pleased Karl Barth and the Barthians and has consequently been a powerful influence in twentieth-century theology. (Claus Westermann, however, has continued to argue for the autonomous character of the creation theology in the book of Genesis.) Within the framework of history, revelation was construed as mediated through word and event rather than through nature. The result of this distinction was a further "disenchantment" of nature (Weber) and a further desacralization of the material world in Christian consciousness.

For a variety of reasons, Roman Catholic theology was less affected by this turn to history. Its preoccupation with the distinction between nature and supernature, and its location of salvific divine action in the sphere of supernature tended to restrict the reference of "nature" to an abstract foil for grace. This preoccupation, however, did as much to "disenchant" nature as the Protestant turn to history was doing. Profound opposition to the notion of divine immanence, together with a rationalistic apologetics that Maurice Blondel stigmatized as "extrinsicism," left Catholic theology disposed to find God active in nature mainly by virtue of working miracles which proved that those in authority in the church had the proper credentials. As George Tyrrell pointed out, the less immanent God is in our thought, the more necessary become God's vice-regents on earth. The Counterreformation church had politically compelling, if not edifying, ecclesiastical reasons for sponsoring transcendence over immanence.[12]

The decisive turn to history came for mainline Roman Catholic theology at and after the second Vatican Council when, having emerged from a largely nonhistorical scholasticism, it discovered salvation history as a master category in a new theological hermeneutics. For many theologians, this hermeneutics represented a major shift of perspective from a pervasive and unchecked essentialism to the existential and relativizing influence of historical consciousness. But it did nothing for the theology of creation. In point of fact Catholic theology, in opening itself to personal, historical, and existentialist modes of thinking, was thereby embracing a fairly luxuriant anthropocentrism. The time has now come to forge a theological anthropology that will place our human species firmly within its natural matrix and therefore recognize that men and women are not the only beneficiaries of God's attention and loving care.

Anthropocentrism is the product of a wide variety of cultural and religious forces. These forces are combined in what Jürgen Moltmann calls "the crisis of domination."[13] Moltmann makes a point of connecting socioeconomic factors with ecological ones. Natural environment cannot be understood apart from social environment:

> The processes which intervene destructively in the natural environment originate in the economic and the social processes. So if the destruction of nature is to be halted, the economic and social conditions of human society must be changed.[14]

I shall return to the socioethical implications of this idea later. Here I wish merely to note the unholy conflation of an anthropocentric theology with a scientific culture that began partly, at least, in the exuberant conviction of Francis Bacon, that knowledge is power, and partly in the passionate belief of Réné Descartes, that the aim of the sciences is to make human beings "masters and possessors of nature."[15] Moltmann is withering in his condemnation of Cartesian dualism because it severs the human being, the *res cogitans*, from nature, the *res extensa*: "Yet to identify the human being as *res cogitans* is just as hostile to his humanity as the subjection of nature to the geometrical notion of extension is hostile to nature."[16] This Cartesian and Baconian mentality has prompted some Christians to interpret Genesis 1:28 and similar biblical texts in an anthropocentric manner—to construe nature as simply for human use and exploitation.

The task that faces contemporary systematic theology is a dialectical one. It has to register the imbalances and distortions we have been considering and redress them as far as possible without going overboard in the opposite direction. A good theology of nature seen as God's creation is not one that outdoes scientistic reductionism by becoming fiercely antihumanist. A good theology of nature sees *homo sapiens* as an integral part of nature but one with spiritual endowments and special obligations. I suggest that the dictum *noblesse oblige* is a realistic motto for the ecological movement, though I am also aware that it is open to misunderstanding.

Translated analogically, it means "rank has its responsibilities." Some may object to the use of the word "rank," since it implies that human beings are higher up the scale than the rest of nature. In terms of biological complexity, to say nothing of self-awareness and freedom, our species is more advanced than any other, and it is disingenuous to pretend otherwise. I am aware that some people may find this observation to be politically incorrect, but I cannot dissemble my conviction that the task before us will never be met by playing down the glory and scandal of being human. I was interested and heartened to read the following words of the United States Catholic Bishops in their statement, *Renewing the Earth*: "We especially call upon Catholic scholars to explore the relationship between this [Catholic] tradition's emphasis upon the dignity of the human person and our responsibility to care for all of God's creation."[17]

In some respects those words articulate our most important task. They place before theologians a fascinating, difficult, and rewarding assignment that can only be undertaken dialectically. Human dignity properly understood is never a threat to the rest of creation. Antihumanism of the kind that denies the special endowments and responsibilities of the human species does nothing for the ecological movement.

A recent ecofeminist study attacks the notion of stewardship as a suitable model for the relationship between human beings and ecology. Anne Primavesi is able to dismiss stewardship as an appropriate symbol of our relationship with the rest of nature because she decides in advance that this model necessarily embodies hierarchical scales of power, value, and control, and is therefore "unecological."[18] This judgment is, however, condemnation by definition. There can be good stewardship and bad stewardship. The word itself is morally neutral and, when used in its favorable sense, is a valuable symbol that enables one to depict participation in the creaturely condition. Yet it also depicts "sufficient transcendence of the creaturely condition" to allow for "caring leadership" as a check to Buber's "leaderless technology" that threatens both civilization and biosphere.[19]

RELATION OF CREATION AND REDEMPTION THEOLOGIES

I come now to the central theme of my paper, namely, an examination of how we might approach the relationship between creation and redemption by taking them as coextensive and mutually interacting. This examination is the most crucial application of the dialectical method. Just as anthropocentrism is not corrected by recourse to a radical antihumanism, neither is creation theology enhanced by a radical rejection of soteriology. Theological truth is best served, here as elsewhere, by a dialectical interplay between two thematic poles—not by the sacrifice of one to the other. Creation is not a mere backdrop to redemption but taken into a process that is continuously both creative and redemptive. The problem is how to work this out in concrete terms.

Two reflections are crucial to my theme: the first deals with the implications of cosmology for our understanding of God as creator; the second, with the implications of evolution for a soteriology that relates closely to nature as creation. I shall argue in both instances that the physical characteristics of nature, human and nonhuman, are relevant—I would go so far as to say indispensable—to a theologically satisfying analysis of God's creation of and action in the world. Science can provide an invaluable corrective to the gnostic tendencies that so easily affect religious thought. I shall assign a nature-derived icon to each of these points.

The Relevance of Cosmology for Understanding God as Creator

I have in my imagination the picture of an intricate design of traceries actually produced in a bubble chamber by colliding subatomic particles.[20] It is an impressive representation of the riotous dance of particles whose movements and interactions are unpredictable except in a broad statistical sense. When color-enhanced, many such photographs become works of abstract art that can be enjoyed purely aesthetically. They may also be used liturgically or as focal points for contemplative prayer.

One result of leaving nature to the scientists is that Christian theology has remained curiously untouched until recently by relativity theory, quantum mechanics, or Hubble's discovery of the red shift, to mention the three great twentieth-century scientific developments that Ernan McMullin has identified as the begetters of modern cosmology. I mention McMullin because he did valuable pioneering work in the history of science and its relevance to theology, and because ten years ago he wrote that theologians on the whole were not disposed to think of cosmology as having much relevance for theology. He made quite clear his conviction that they were rather remiss in this notion.[21]

The situation is, I think, changing, largely as the result of the need theologians feel to make an appropriate response to the ecological crisis. Most theologians (and I am among them) are not professionally competent as scientists. But we cannot afford to make scientific incompetence an excuse for not taking a subject like cosmology with theological seriousness. Fortunately, there are professional scientists writing for the general reader, just as there are professional scientists who are also practicing theologians.

Ian Barbour has pointed out that "our understanding of God's relation to nature always reflects our view of nature."[22] Neither the Ptolemaic, nor the Copernican, nor the Newtonian universe lent itself to a theology of divine presence or sustained action in the world. Indeed, Newton's universe seems tailor-made for deistic absenteeism (mitigated, perhaps, by an occasional divine visit to shore up a sagging planetary orbit here or to rectify the direction of a wayward comet there). Nature now revealed to us through quantum theory and evolutionary biology is a strange blend of unpredictable and random events of a statistical regularity sufficient to allow one to speak of its laws.

Niels Bohr, echoing Augustine's reflection on the mind in search of God, remarked that those who were not shocked when they first came across quantum physics could not possibly have understood it.[23] One appreciates his point. Literally unimaginable indeterminate smudges of energy wait to be observed in order to achieve concrete existence. The observer is part of the observed phenomenon. Yet observation is limited to mutually exclusive modes: you can determine the position of an electron but only at the expense of the inability to measure or observe its momentum. The subatomic world is composed of potentialities whose actualization is not predetermined except in a broad statistical sense. Subatomic particles are not individual solitary entities but belong to a system within which they interact mysteriously and unpredictably with each other. It now appears that fideistic believers are not the only ones saying "Credo quia absurdum." One does not have to be a Kierkegaardian to embrace paradox; particle physicists are doing it every day.

This new humility imposed by events on scientists has led to a general perking up on the part of theologians who realize what is happening, though whether shared epistemological discomfort is a sound basis for interdisciplinary cooperation is questionable.

Newtonian determinism was a major casualty of the new physics. Pierre de Laplace had claimed that if the position and motion of every particle in the universe were known with exactitude at one instant it would be possible to compute the entire past and future history of the universe.[24] Laplace's appalling thesis remains attractive to some scientific minds when faced with phenomena that resist rational explanation just as its theological equivalent has often been invoked by believers who want to ascribe every event to the direct intervention of God.

On the other hand, it is easy to appreciate why theologians of a different cast of mind may warm to quantum theory. When Heisenberg remarks that "even in science the object of research is no longer nature itself, but man's investigation of nature,"[25] he sounds so like Schleiermacher and the liberal Protestant tradition that one cannot help wondering whimsically whether physics will throw up a scientific equivalent of Karl Barth to call it back from its Copenhagen exile. In the meantime we can rejoice in a God who is apparently happy to be creative, at microscopic and macroscopic levels, through the instrumentality of an elegant interplay between chance and necessity.[26]

Another benefit of the new physics is that by promoting holistic thinking it acts as a powerful corrective to the deadening reductionism endemic in certain types of scientific thought. In addition, it has bequeathed to theology the heuristic and hermeneutical device of the model, which allows one to practice negative theology without having to take a vow of total silence. This may or may not be thought a blessing, but it is an undeniable fact of theological life, at least in the English-speaking world.

Some theologians have actually applied Niels Bohr's theory of complementarity to the classical christological and trinitarian doctrines. Here, however, it would be wise to heed John Hedley Brooke in his *Science and Religion*, when he warns us against incautious use of the new physics by theologians. Complementarity in physics applies to two descriptions of the same phenomenon, each of which is complete in itself though exclusive of the other when measured or observed: "To switch from complementarity at the same level to complementarity between different levels (especially if one involved the transcendent) [is] not a straightforward move."[27]

There is also the danger of circular argument. Bohr liked to draw on psychology and philosophy for support of his scientific theory. For example, he drew on William James's notion of the stream of consciousness: if you try to examine the stream of consciousness it ceases, by that very fact, to be the object you want to examine. Bohr also took inspiration from Kierkegaard's protest against the objectivizing effect of scientism and Hegelianism. Human beings are subjects not objects. Brooke comments dryly:

> With so rich an input into the Copenhagen interpretation of quantum mechanics, it is not surprising that religious apologists should obtain an output. But the danger of circularity is transparent.[28]

What cosmology forces on the theologian's attention is the inherently insoluble problem of the mode of God's action in the world. Here, if anywhere, negative theology rules. It is not a Laplacean lack of relevant evidence or an insufficiently evolved brain power that makes this an intrinsically insoluble problem. Recognition of our inability to understand God's action in causal terms is an integral and scandalizing feature of faith. Yet denying that there is any efficient causality in God's relationship with the world on the grounds that efficient causality necessarily trenches on freedom or is unacceptably patriarchal is, I think, unreal. Causality thus banished inevitably returns under another name. Surely it is better to accept the paradox of affirming both divine causality on the one hand and chance and freedom on the other. There seems little to be gained by making the word "creation" theologically correct while banishing the word "cause" as theologically unacceptable. Instead, given that models have become a fact of theological life, we may as well lay on a plentiful supply of them on the grounds, as Ian Ramsey liked to say, of safety in numbers.

It may very well be that Process philosophy, in one or other of its forms, is a necessary, if perhaps temporary, stage in the journey from undue reliance on essentialist, existentialist, or historicist types of theological thinking. At any rate, it would appear that many theologians with a professional scientific background have a marked interest in Process thought. Ian Barbour notes that Process thought is "particularly compatible" with modern cosmology since it is disposed to see "reality [as] constituted by events and relationships rather than by separate substances or separate particles."[29] It is holistic and sees nature in relational terms, and it makes becoming rather than being a central category of its thinking. Some theologians are uneasy about its affirmation that creation belongs to the nature of God. Others see its thesis of bipolarity as trying to have one's cake and eat it. Still others take issue with its rejection of creation *ex nihilo* and its substitution of creation out of chaos.

One of the attractive features of Process thought is that it gives nearly everybody something to disagree with. Nevertheless, taking cosmology with theological seriousness makes it virtually impossible to avoid engaging with Process thought, however guardedly.

Redeeming Creation

The icon I have chosen for introducing my reflection on the relationship between creation and redemption comes from my country Ireland. On the Dingle Peninsula in County Kerry stands the Gallarus Oratory, a tiny dry-stone church built in the eighth century. It stands in the midst of wild and beautiful countryside bounded by the Atlantic Ocean. The building itself is totally without adornment—in fact, it looks rather like a stack of turf—but it has stood there for something like twelve hundred years, a constant reminder of the monks who built it for their worship. They were known for the austerity of their lives and for their love of nature.

Some years ago the poet Seamus Heaney visited the oratory and experienced "a kind of small epiphany." Later, in a radio talk on early Irish nature poetry entitled, "The God in the Tree," Heaney described that epiphany.

> Inside, in the dark of the stone, it feels as if you are sustaining a great pressure, bowing under like the generations of monks who must have bowed down in meditation and reparation on that floor.

I felt the weight of Christianity in all its rebuking aspects, its calls to self-denial and self-abnegation, its humbling of the proud flesh and insolent spirit. But coming out of the cold heart of the stone, into the sunlight and the dazzle of grass and sea, I felt a lift in my heart, a surge towards happiness that must have been experienced over and over again by those monks as they crossed that same threshold centuries ago. This surge towards praise, this sudden apprehension of the world as light, as illumination, this is what remains central to our first nature poetry and makes it a unique inheritance.[30]

A feel for nature and its beauties was a feature of Celtic monasticism in spite of its apparently world-denying asceticism. It is as if in renouncing the attractions and pleasures of the world, these monks found in nature a reflection of the beauty of God. Many of us would doubtless find much in their spirituality difficult to accommodate, but their attitude to nature has never seemed more relevant than it does today.

I see in Gallarus Oratory, taken in its natural setting, a symbol of the relationship between creation and redemption. Heaney's evocation of the leap of heart, which the monks must have experienced on emerging from the oratory into the open air, is a warning, should we need it, against too easy a distinction between nature and grace—as though the peninsula symbolizes nature; the oratory, grace. Who shall say that the sight of the green grass and the flash of white waves upon the Atlantic Ocean were not for those early medieval monks as much a manifestation of God's Spirit as the psalms and canticles of the prayer book they recited in the chapel?

The oratory and the countryside neatly symbolize a relationship that others would present as mutually exclusive, thereby forcing us to choose between them. Some authors, for example, go out of their way to draw up lists in parallel columns. One column represents the dark, repressive, joyless elements of redemption-centered theology; the other, the bright, enabling, joyful elements of creation-centered theology. A great deal more would have to be known about these monks and what they thought they were doing, both in the oratory and by their chosen way of life, before we can be in a position to decide how they related their penitential exercises to their love of nature. Heaney is right to note the contrast between the oratory and its natural environment, as he is subtle in his suggestion of some sort of complementarity between them.

If a theology of creation is to have credibility it must reckon realistically with the lament and blame of evil. Deliberately to avoid this issue is to fall into a facile romanticism.[31] In much of nature, evil is present as lament, for example, in animal suffering. Evil as blame is possible only in human beings in whom the relationship between evil as wrongdoing and evil as suffering are often intertwined in a disturbingly ambiguous way. An ecologically sensitive theology will notice the instances in which animal suffering is a result of human sinfulness. A connection with redemption can also be established: with appropriate conversion, the redeemed man or woman can be seen as one who cares for creation.

The process of our rethinking our relationship to nature begins with an affirmation of our oneness with it. This means correcting significant elements of the existentialist heritage that played such an important role first in Protestantism and then in Catholic theology during and after the second Vatican Council. Think, for example, of Rudolf Bultmann's remark that history is the history of mankind and that humanity is not a part of the cosmos but is fundamentally separate from the world.[32] Or think of Karl Rahner's no more acceptable opinion that the world "is seen correctly . . . not as 'holy nature', but as the material for the creative power of man."[33]

Even more serious is the stance taken by John Macquarrie in his influential book, *Principles of Christian Theology*. Macquarrie is impenitent in his anthropocentrism: "Our first step toward an interpretation of the doctrine of creation is to take man himself rather than nature as the paradigm of creaturely beings."[34] He quotes Rahner with "profound agreement": "It is at men above all that we must look in order to learn what the Creator-creature relationship is."[35]

Macquarrie fears the very feature that I wish to promote here, namely, a real involvement with the physical character of nature; he finds in Existentialism a valuable alternative to an approach to creation through nature that "can so easily become the question of how things began and can trespass into an area that properly belongs to science."[36] The warning is well taken. We have no warrant, for example, to take the Big Bang as the moment of creation in the theological sense. But this fear of "dangerous" involvement with science can seriously inhibit the development of a theology of creation that can serve adequately as a foundation for environmental theology. Some dangers have to be risked, especially when it becomes necessary to correct an imbalance in an overall theological presentation.

When we human beings affirm our authentic presence in the world and seek to exercise our graced freedom there, it is nature that is doing it in us, for it is through natural processes that we have emerged into humanized nature. In *us* nature groans for redemption. We cannot have it both ways: we cannot assert that the human species is part of nature and at the same time place that species over against nature. If men and women need redemption, nature can properly be said to need redemption. I find in that thought the basis for a fruitful interpretation of the concept of "new creation."

Taking evolution with the seriousness it deserves is the most effective way of affirming our oneness with nature. Recognition of what Michael Polanyi calls "anthropogenesis" does not mean that we have capitulated to anthropocentrism.[37] Indeed I would argue that the contrary is the case. Recognition of our physical, chemical, and biological origins is the best safeguard against anthropocentric arrogance. If I were to suggest an icon at this point, it would be the picture of chimpanzees with a caption announcing that these delightful creatures have a DNA structure nearly the same as our human one. For creationists and supernaturalists, this icon may be a salutary, if painful, thought. By the same token, reductionists might be invited to reflect that similarity in molecular structure is only part of the story.

Benjamin Disraeli was both theologically and scientifically gauche when, in 1864 (i.e., five years after the publication of Darwin's *The Origin of Species* and four years before he became British Prime Minister), at a meeting of the Society for Increasing Endowments of Small Livings in the Diocese of Oxford, he asked with a rhetorical flourish carefully calculated to gratify his audience: "Is man an ape or an angel? Now I am on the side of the angels."[38] Evolutionary theory is supported by a vast amount of empirical evidence; it cannot with impunity be dismissed as theologically irrelevant or, what is possibly worse, be accepted with bad grace and a purely theoretical assent with no practical consequences. The choice to be made is not between ape and angel: the harder and truer choice is to discern the mystery of their combination in one species.

While it is scientifically implausible to deny the evolutionary continuity between *homo sapiens* and earlier forms of life, it is sheer philistinism to deny the element of discontinuity that is also evident. The difference between our species and the other primates may be minute in molecular terms, but it is striking in holistic and cultural terms. The biologist Charles Birch puts this point trenchantly:

> It is not that the whole is more than the sum of the parts, but that its parts themselves are redefined and recreated in the process of evolution from one level to another. An electron in a lump of lead is not the same as an electron in a cell in a human brain.[39]

Birch shows incidentally how essentialism is almost inevitably mechanistic in its vision of the world. When we remember how deeply Catholic dogma has been stamped by essentialist ways of thinking, Birch's observation is particularly to the point.

> In substance-thinking the substance is independent of relations and then enters into relations which are always external ones. In the ecological model [on the other hand] internal relations are constitutive of the entity.[40]

This thought, coupled with a soundly worked out theology of divine immanence in the world, could provide a solid base in systematic theology for an ecologically sensitive theology. It could also help us incorporate a realistic estimate of the presence of evil into our vision of the cosmos and our relationship with it, thus establishing a significant link between creation and redemption.

Holistic thinking is not merely about intrasystemic relationships; it is also about the breakup of previous unities precisely that these relationships may be formed. This breakup of unities occurs all the way through nature from subatomic particles to human social relationships. For theological reasons, I prefer the term "alienation" to characterize the process. In its literal etymological sense, alienation simply means "making other." As such it names a natural and morally neutral process. It can, of course, also refer to much more complicated and programmatic relationships and as such it is used by Hegelians, Marxists, Freudians, and Existentialists. Its Christian reference is immediately clear when it is used as a synonym for sin and related antithetically to reconciliation as a root soteriological metaphor. The two words "alienation" and "reconciliation" are correlative and can be read with an imagination that is at home with pluralism and ambiguity. That a process which in nonhuman nature is ethically neutral takes on an ethical reference when brought within the sphere of self-awareness, sociolinguistic relationships, and the operations of conscience, is as John Henry Newman noted, a connecting principle between the creature and the creator.[41]

One can think analogically of systemic relationships as the "reconciliation" of fractured unities of any kind in nature, whether or not they have ethical reference. In the evolutionary process, each break with a previous unity results in a more complex organization of the original materials, which in turn makes possible a further complexification. Once we arrive at sentient beings, hurt and pain become part of the very process that allows ever greater freedom until we arrive at our own species *homo sapiens* with its awesome powers for both good and evil. At this point the alienation that is systemic in nature has made relationships possible that were not possible before and which are profoundly significant at the linguistic, moral, and religious level on which we have to cope with both moral delinquency and tragedy—often at the same time.

To introduce another icon: we are a species that builds hospitals and concentration camps. We are a species that can make the desert bloom. By the same token we are a species that also reduces blooms to deserts.

Traditional precritical theology accounted for the coexistence of good and evil within the human person and within human societies by its doctrine of the fall. For many reasons, the precritical understanding of "original sin" with its reliance on a literal interpretation of the book of Genesis is not a plausible option for many contemporary Christian theologians. Nevertheless the human phenomenon for which the doctrine of original sin was advanced as a mythical articulation is, and always will be, with us. Reinterpretation of the doctrine is an urgent theological task if the reality it sought to describe and account for is not to be simply ignored by those who quite properly reject the literalized mythology and the confusion of theological models on which the traditional doctrine was based.[42]

My contention is that such a reinterpretation can best be brought about by recognizing the evolutionary context of nature and by using one's historical imagination to contemplate its progress along a line of expanding possibilities, which, in our own human species, have become ethical and religious in addition to being natural. (In this connection I believe that it is necessary to be on one's guard against attacks on the nature/culture distinction. That this distinction can be ideologically misused is not a sufficient reason for rejecting it.) Something enormously significant happens to nature as it evolves into human expression. If it is to achieve its divinely willed destiny, nature as it expresses itself in human culture, has to open itself to a radical process of reshaping and being reshaped, of healing and being healed, of reconciling and being reconciled, that in traditional theological language is called salvation or redemption.

Creation is indeed an original blessing that always comes to human beings, because of their freedom, with the possibility of refusal, and the possibility has, of course, become an actuality. As a species we have, on a significant scale, refused to cooperate with the creator. In theological terms, redemption is not discontinuous with creation; it is not a redesign initiative on God's part. Redemption is God's answer to the human refusal to cooperate with God's creative purposes. So far from being a joyless, life-denying, patriarchically inspired exercise in the expiation of guilt, redemption is God's life-affirming assurance that no degree of human viciousness or stupidity shall be allowed to subvert the divine creative purposes. Creation is a divine adventure attended by constant risk and prompted by inextinguishable love. The critique of patriarchy is a powerful reminder that, in recognizing and proclaiming God's sovereignty over all nature, we have sometimes drawn the false conclusion that omnipotence and sovereignty necessarily mean control. Creation no less than redemption is a kenotic act. As John Macquarrie puts it, "In creating, [God] consents to know the pain and frustration of the world."[43] God's love for creation is expressed in a profound respect for its autonomy and, in the case of human beings, its freedom. Real and unfeigned respect for the freedom of others is a costly business not only for human beings but also for God.

IMPLICATIONS OF A REFURBISHED CREATION THEOLOGY

In the last section of my paper I wish to consider how the theology of creation may be related to other branches of theology. Though I must obviously be selective and brief in my treatment, I single out for slightly more developed attention two areas in which creation theology intersects with practical theology: liberation and ecumenism and ecofeminism.

Ecological Theology Related to
Solidarity with the Poor and to Ecumenism

First, I wish to establish a link between systematic, practical, and ecumenical theology. It is instructive to follow the pattern of events that led the World Council of Churches (WCC) from its initial "christocentric universalism" (W. A. Visser 't Hooft) through its option for the poor and oppressed to its present concern with ecological matters. The progression has not been successive but cumulative—with consequent and serious internal stresses and strains. In March 1960, sixty-seven black South Africans were killed by the police at Sharpville. The massacre politicized a significant segment of the WCC, and a lively debate followed. In 1969, the WCC set up its Programme to Combat Racism. As one observer remarks, "The WCC would never be the same again: it had taken sides with the racially oppressed."[44]

However, the WCC's engagement with the oppressed and the poor brought it face-to-face with other unavoidable questions connected with development. The notion of sustainability entered the WCC vocabulary in the 1970s; in 1975 the Fifth Assembly, meeting in Nairobi, produced a theme that has been unfolding ever since, namely, the search for a just, participatory, and sustainable society. Sustainability is a concept derived from the recognition that there are limits to growth. The Brundtland Report, *Our Common Future* (1987), defines sustainability as the kind of development that allows us to meet our current needs without trespassing on the rights of future generations to enjoy the same access to the world's natural wealth. At the Sixth Assembly of the WCC in Vancouver in 1983, the theme was given the form it has today: "Justice, Peace and the Integrity of Creation." This theme was a daring progression; it combined three separate themes in a unified program in search of a difficult theological coherence that many would say has not yet been achieved.

In fact, the debates that took place in the WCC between Vancouver (1983) and Canberra (1991) revealed a field of tension that exists throughout the developing world. Ecological concern is easily seen, especially by committed workers for justice, as an aesthetic indulgence on the part of the affluent. Konrad Raiser, a former deputy general secretary of the WCC, in his important book *Ecumenism in Transition*,[45] speaks of a still unresolved difference of approach: "The new commitment to the 'integrity of creation' stands over against the continuing obligation to struggle for 'justice'." He goes on to ask the uncomfortable question:

> Is there behind the environmental commitment and the ecological movements of the industrialized nations a latent evasion of the demands for social and economic justice throughout the world?

This question will have to be kept constantly in mind, especially by theologians not working directly out of a liberation experience. It is, for example, easy for the developed world to call for saving the great life-teeming forests of the tropics without making a simultaneous commitment to reimburse poor nations who cooperate in preserving these forests and other ecologically responsible projects.

One other connection between the theology of creation and the ecumenical movement deserves mention. It is widely accepted today that the movement is in need of rejuvenation.[46] Per Lønning, an experienced ecumenical theologian, suggests that widening the ecumenical agenda to include the theology of creation may inject new life into the movement for Christian unity. He sees it as an area in which interfaith dialogue could feed back into interchurch dialogue. The methodological principle is simple but important: dialogue with other faiths can alert us to elements in our own faith that we have neglected. Nature-orientated cultures and religions have much to say to Christians about the first article of the Christian creed on God as creator.[47]

Ecofeminism

The other area in which creation theology intersects with practical theology is now commonly called "ecofeminism." Nobody working in critical theology today can be unaffected by the dynamic radicalism of feminist theology. The combination of feminism and ecological concern is a potent one indeed. As long ago as 1975, Rosemary Ruether wrote:

Women must see that there can be no liberation for them and no solution to the ecological crisis within a society whose fundamental model of relationships continues to be one of domination.[48]

The critique of patriarchy is a central element in feminism quite apart from its association with ecology. Ecofeminism extends the application of this critique to male attitudes to nature. This sobering charge needs to be registered by systematic as well as practical theologians. Lois K. Daly claims, however, that "ecofeminism is not just another branch of feminism."[49] She sees ecofeminism as transcending the differences between social feminism, which rejects the identification of women with nature, and nature feminism, which affirms this identification but denies "that nature or the physical is inferior."[50] For many male theologians, Sallie McFague's *Models of God* has proved to be a valuable entry to feminist thinking about God and God's relationship to the world.[51] Because of her work in the methodology of theological models, McFague offers a foothold to theologians who have some familiarity with the critique of models but are still wrestling with the more disturbing implications of feminist theology.

Other Areas of Systematic Theology

Christology, ecclesiology, and sacramental theology are particularly open to development in the light of a renewed creation theology. Each calls for the sort of extended treatment that is beyond the scope of this paper. Here I shall restrict myself to a brief comment on each. Theologians who are conscious of the need for a creation dimension in their christological thought will probably wish to explore the Pauline model of the cosmic Christ, going on perhaps to examine Pierre Teilhard's thesis that "Christ must, without losing his precise humanity, become co-extensive with the physical expanse of time and space."[52]

It goes without saying that the feminist and ecological critiques of patriarchy have far-reaching implications for ecclesiology. This question is so large and, for many Catholics in today's church, so dispiriting that I leave it with a sense of temporary relief, contenting myself with the suggestion that a creation-conscious ecclesiology would explore the notion of church as a gathering of people who frequently celebrate nature as God's gift.

This suggestion immediately links the church with liturgy and the sacraments. A host of icons come to mind here. The *Didache* long ago associated the wheat field and the vineyard with the Eucharist. Perhaps this association could be made again in eucharistic theology and liturgical practice. Each of the sacraments uses natural products, such as water, oil, bread, and wine. The theology of the sacraments could devote more attention to these products and relate them specifically to the natural world from which they come. Using the sacramental principle, but extending its scope beyond the seven sacraments, liturgists might design prayer services with the specific purpose of celebrating nature as creation. To take one instance, Roman Catholics, at least in some parts of Europe, seem to leave harvest festivals to Anglicans, thereby forfeiting a magnificent opportunity to celebrate and express gratitude for the produce of nature. Harvesting is a potent symbol in Christian thought, while the farmer is symbolic of our general attitude to nature. The problems that farmers are facing all over the world are symptomatic of a deep-seated human malaise that makes market forces the only determinant of how we treat the earth.

CONCLUSION

In this paper I have considered some features in the history of Western Christian theology that have contributed to a long neglect of creation notably a preoccupation with divine transcendence at the expense of immanence, a recourse to history as the predominant category for considering God's dealings with creation, an emphasis on the supernatural at the expense of the natural, an accentuation of the exclusively human, and the reduction of creation to the status of mere backdrop to redemption. But I have also argued against any kind of antihumanism as a reaction to the undoubted anthropocentrism of traditional Christian theology. I suggest that the physical characteristics of nature as revealed by science are material to a sound theology of creation, including a realistic evaluation of what has been traditionally referred to as original sin. The theology of creation can and must be related to the other branches of theology.

At several points in this paper I have drawn on what I describe as nature-derived icons. The ones I have chosen are but samples taken from a large storehouse that is open to any imagination in search of ways of thinking and talking about God. The mere fact of placing in a church one such picture—for example, the earth as seen from space—would be an instant reminder of the doctrine of creation and also of our religious and ethical responsibilities to nature.

I am, of course, suggesting an analogy with the icons of the Eastern Church. There are obvious differences, and one striking similarity: the icon has been traditionally seen as a "window on the divine." An image taken from nature can perform the same function if the imagination is primed to see God in what God has brought into being.

I close with an image provided by the poet, Cecil Day Lewis, as he remembers the day his son first left for school. Many parents have gone through the experience, but Day Lewis gives it transcendent reference.

I have had worse partings, but none that so
Gnaws at my mind still. Perhaps it is roughly
Saying what God alone could perfectly show—
How selfhood begins with a walking away,

And love is proved in the letting go.[53]

Although the image is human it can stand for the cosmos. It catches much of the ambiguity and ambivalence of alienation. The entire creative process is a walking away from simple to more complex systemic relationships. A unity is fractured so that new relationships may be born. Nothing is lost in the process: the earlier is taken up into the later. When human beings walk out into self-awareness and a new kind of freedom, they take with them the dust of the earth from which they are formed. The ecological crisis is a powerful reminder of the challenges and responsibilities that go with being both ape and angel.

NOTES

1. R. Grant and D. Tracy, *A Short History of the Interpretation of the Bible* (London: SCM Press, 1984), 170; D. Tracy, *Blessed Rage for Order: The New Pluralism in Theology* (San Francisco: Harper Row, 1975), 32–34; W. Jeanrond. *Theological Hermeneutics: Development and Significance* (New York: Crossroad, 1991). 174–76.

2. Cited in K. W. Kelley, *The Home Planet* (London: McDonald Queen Anne Press, 1988), No. 45.

3. J. Lovelock, *The Ages of Gaia: A Biography of Our Living Earth* (Oxford: Oxford University Press, 1989), 41.

4. S. Schneiders, *Beyond Patching: Faith and Feminism in the Catholic Church* (New York: Paulist Press, 1991), 37–71. This book offers some valuable hermeneutical insights into ways of reading the Bible as God's word while being painfully aware of its patriarchal attitudes and language. See also S. Schneiders, *The Revelatory Text: Interpreting the New Testament as Sacred Scripture.* (San Francisco: Harper, 1991).

5. See J. A. Baker, "Biblical views of Nature," in *Liberating life: Contemporary Approaches to Ecological Theology,* ed. C. Birch et al. (New York: Orbis, 1990), 9–26.

6.   P. Gregorios, *Cosmic Man: The Divine Presence*. (Geneva: World Council of Churches, 1980), 184, 210–18.

7.   J. Cobb and D. Griffin. *Process Theology: An Introductory Exposition* (Belfast: Christian Journals, 1977), 8–10.

8.   J. Moltmann. *History and the Triune God: Contributions to Trinitarian Theology* (London: SCM Press, 1991), *passim*, but especially xi–xix; W. Kasper, *The God of Jesus Christ* (New York: Crossroad, 1988), *passim*, but especially 233–316; L. Boff. *Trinity and Society* (Tunbridge Wells, England: Burns and Oats, 1988), *passim*, but especially 213–31. See also G. Daly. "A response to Walter Kasper" *Irish Theological Quarterly*. 55(2): 114–24.

9.   C. J. M. Halkes, *New Creation: Christian Feminism and the Renewal of the Earth* (London: SPCK, 1991), 78.

10.   A Schloz, "Misleading Alternatives," in *Reintegrating God's Creation* (Geneva: World Council of Churches, 1987), 15.

11.   Cited in B. M. G. Reardon, *Liberal Protestantism*. (London: A & C Black, 1968), 126.

12.   G. Tyrrell, *Through Scylla and Charybdis: Or the Old Theology and the New* (London: Longmans, 1907), 359–60, 363–65. Tyrrell is extremely perceptive in drawing attention to the link between the absence of an immanent dimension in one's theology of creation and absolutism in one's conception of church government. The point might be developed with profit by theologians who today are combating patriarchy.

13.   J. Moltmann, *God in Creation: An Ecological Doctrine of Creation* (London: SCM Press, 1985), 23.

14.   Ibid., 23–24.

15.   Ibid., 27.

16.   Ibid.

17.   *Origins*, 21(27): 432.

18.   A. Primavesi, *From Apocalypse to Genesis: Ecology, Feminism and Christianity* (Tunbridge Wells, England: Burns & Oats, 1991), 106–7.

19.   See D. J. Hall, "The Integrity of Creation: Biblical and Theological Background of the Term," in *Reintegrating God's Creation*, 34. The New Testament uses the word "steward" in both its favorable and unfavorable senses. Any Christian theologian who wished to define it in an exclusively pejorative sense would need to take account of Luke 12:42, 1 Corinthians 4:1–2, Titus 1:7, 1 Peter 4:10.

20.   The particular photograph I have in mind is reproduced in F. Close, et al., eds. *The Particle Explosion*. (Oxford: Oxford University Press, 1987), 129. The field for choice is, of course, limitless.

21.   E. McMullin, "How Should Cosmology Relate to Theology?" in *The Sciences and Theology in the Twentieth Century*, ed. A. R. Peacocke (Stocksfield, England: Oriel Press, 1981), 17.

22.   I. Barbour, *Religion in an Age of Science* (London: SCM, 1990), 183.

23.   See Barbour, 95–101 for a succinct comment on quantum theory.

24.   C. Kaiser, *Creation and the History of Science* (London: Marshall Pickering, 1991), 267–69.

25. J. H. Brooke, *Science and Religion: Some Historical Perspectives* (Cambridge: Cambridge University Press, 1991), 334.

26. See D. J. Bartholomew, *God of Chance* (London: SCM, 1984); A. R. Peacocke, *Theology for a Scientific Age: Being and Becoming—Natural and Divine* (Oxford: Blackwell, 1990), 115–21.

27. Brooke, *Science and Religion*, 331.

28. Ibid., 333.

29. Barbour, *Religion in an Age of Science*, 221.

30. S. Heaney, *Preoccupations: Select Prose 1968-1978* (London: Faber & Faber, 1984), 189.

31. The distinction between evil as lament and evil as blame is made forcefully by Paul Ricoeur who draws attention to the ambiguity of the word "evil": "The whole enigma of evil may be said to lie in the fact that, at least in the traditions of the West, we put under the same terms such different phenomena as sin, suffering, and death. However, evil as wrongdoing and evil as suffering belong to two heterogenous categories, that of blame and that of lament" (in "Evil, a Challenge to Philosophy and Theology," *Trajectories in the Study of Religion: Addresses at the Seventy-fifth Anniversary of the American Academy of Religion*, ed. R. L. Hart (Atlanta: Scholars Press, 1987), 68).

32. Cited in Halkes, *New Creation*, 79.

33. K. Rahner, *Foundations of Christian Faith: An Introduction to the Idea of Christianity* (London: Daston, Longsman and Todd, 1978), 80–81.

34. J. Macquarrie, *Principles of Christian Theology*. Revised edition (London: SCM Press, 1977), 212.

35. MacQuarrie, *Principles*, 213, citing Karl Rahner, *Theological Investigations* 1 trans. Kevin Smyth, (Baltimore: Helicon Press, 1966).

36. MacQuarry, *Principles*, 216.

37. M. Polanyi, *Personal knowledge: Towards a Post-Critical Philosophy* (London: Routledge & Kegan Paul, 1973), 385–90. In these pages and elsewhere, Polanyi refers to evolution in relation to humankind as an *emergence* from bacillus to noosphere. On page 393, he asks: "How can the emergent have arisen from particulars that cannot constitute it? Does some new creative agent enter the emergent system at every new stage? If so, how can we account for the continuity of the process of anthropogenesis?" These questions are as relevant to theology as they are to anthropology though with the warning of existentialists ringing in our ears we may be chary of the notion that a creative agent enters the system at every new stage.

38. *The Concise Oxford Dictionary of Quotations* (Oxford: Oxford University Press, 1981), 86.

39. C. Birch, *On Purpose* (Kensington, New South Wales: New South Wales University Press, 1990), 44.

40. Ibid., 75.

41. J. H. Newman, *An Essay in Aid of a Grammar of Assent* (London: Longman's, 1895), 117.

42. See G. Daly, *Creation and Redemption* (Wilmington: Michael Glazier, 1989), 114–47.

43. J. Macquarrie, *In Search of Deity: An Essay in Dialectical Theism* (London: SCM Press, 1984), 180.

44. B. Sjollema, "Programme to Combat Racism," in N. Lossky et al., eds. *Dictionary of the Ecumenical Movement* (Geneva: World Council of Churches, 1991), 827. Sjollema continues:

Charity was being replaced by solidarity. The WCC became more relevant to the majority of Christians and even to people of other faiths. Concrete action against racism had severely tested the ecumenical fellowship, but it was not broken (ibid).

45. K. Raiser, *Ecumenism in Transition: A Paradigm Shift in the Ecumenical Movement?* (Geneva: World Council of Churches, 1991), 68.

46. Reporting to the Assembly at Canberra in 1991, General Secretary Emilio Castro noted "a lack of ardour and impatience. "It is taken for granted that we cannot get beyond our confessional divisions." M. Kinnamon, ed. *Signs of the Spirit: Official Report of the Seventh Assembly.* (Geneva: World Council of Churches, 1991), 166.

47. P. Lønning, *Creation—An Ecumenical Challenge: Reflections Issuing from a Study of the Institute for Ecumenical Research, Strasbourg, France* (Macon, Georgia: Mercer University Press, 1989), 72.

48. R. Ruether, *New Woman, New Earth: Sexist Ideologies and Human Liberation* (New York: Seabury, 1975), 204.

49. L. K. Daly, Ecofeminism, Reverence for Life, and Feminist Theological Ethics, in *Liberating Life*, eds. C. Birch et al., 92–93.

50. Ibid., 91–92.

51. S. McFague, *Models of God: Theology for an Ecological, Nuclear Age* (Philadelphia: Fortress Press, 1987).

52. P. Teilhard de Chardin, *Human Energy* (London: Collins, 1969), 91. I have discussed some christological aspects of creation in *Creation and Redemption*, 75–113.

53. *Poems of C. Day Lewis* (London: Cape, 1977), 234.

Powerful Icons and Missing Pieces

ELIZABETH A. JOHNSON, C.S.J.

We owe a debt of thanks to Professor Gabriel Daly for the new insights expressed in his paper and for the icons with which he illuminated those ideas. The paper is a tour de force, comprehensive in scope and challenging in its ramifications. Its depth and lyrical quality make us realize that Ireland is still an island of poets and scholars.

Returning creation to the center of theological reflection, seeing it as not merely a backdrop for the history of salvation but as co-extensive and mutually interacting with redemption—this is surely an important move for an ecological theology. So, too, is discourse about God's creation that starts from the physical data provided by contemporary science. This interface between theology and the natural sciences, seen again in Professor Daly's retrieval of original sin within an evolutionary view of the world, is a methodological step of major importance. In fact, the contribution of Professor Daly's paper, as I see it, is his demonstration that classical Catholic doctrine has the potential to contribute richly to a new, sorely needed development of religious thinking in an age of environmental crisis. Like the biblical householder of old, he has brought out of the storeroom of faith things new and old and set them in conversation with a new partner.

In response I will (1) press his view of theological foundations on an issue of method; (2) draw attention to a crucial doctrinal concept touched on only briefly; (3) raise four critical questions relative to particular points; and (4) end with a practical suggestion.

First, the foundational issue. Near the end of his paper Professor Daly alludes to the link that feminist thinkers have made between male domination of women and the earth. The point is well taken, but the implications are more profound than he has credited and affect the theological work in the body of his paper.

The ecofeminist critique of patriarchy does not stop with saying that patriarchy is a factor in bad ecological attitudes and practice, which it indeed is. Rather, feminist theological analysis reveals that patriarchy is a governing factor in bad *theology* as well. It has distorted fundamental assumptions that shape the Christian doctrines of creation, redemption, and original sin in their classical form, along with the idea of the Creator God in relation to the world. Patriarchy is a foundational issue as well as a practical one. Unless we look clearly at this critique, we have not gotten to a major root of the religious problem.

Christian theology emerged in the context of hellenistic thought and adopted the strong form of gender dualism characteristic of Greek philosophy. The ecologically problematic vision of "man" over nature that undergirds traditional theology is, in fact, an expression of this ancient polarized pattern of thought which divides spirit from matter, mind from body, reason from feeling, culture from nature, and so forth. The two spheres thus divided are not of equal value but are ranked in a hierarchial manner, the first of each pair being the more important and "godly." It does not escape women's attention today that the first of each pair is identified with the male principle in the universe and the second with the female.

According to this world view, actual women, whose bodies create and nourish physical existence, are lined up with matter, passions, and nature in a way opposed to spirit, reason, and culture. When values are assigned, women, the body, and nature are the lower half of this dualism. They are declared subject to men and their autonomy or intrinsic worth is denigrated insofar as they are assigned a subservient purpose in life. This purpose, it is assumed, is to be at the service of men who rule by right since they alone are fully in the image of God (if we take Augustine, Aquinas, and a host of other male theologians at their face value).

It is thus no accident that nature is symbolized as female; that the domination of nature is compared with the domination of a wife; that investigation into nature is compared with inquisitorial interrogation of female witches with instruments of torture (Francis Bacon); that the exploitation of nature is portrayed in analogy with the rape of a woman. In truth, what Professor Daly critiques as an overly anthropocentric theology is actually an androcentric theology. What he speaks about as human dominance is actually the dominance of a ruling male elite.[1]

Historically, symbolically, and conceptually the social injustice carried out in man's subordination of woman functions as the paradigm of man's domination of nature. When seen together with racism, classism, and militarism, sexism and ecological destructiveness are intrinsically connected aspects of patriarchal consciousness and praxis. To express this with yet another icon: patriarchy is like a drowned continent shaping all theological currents that swirl around it in the ocean, though it is invisible and most often ignored. To move from the idea and practice of dominating exploitation to mutuality and interdependence with the earth, this distorted form of relationship must be critiqued and dismantled even in theology. To overlook this linchpin at the very center of the problem leaves one open yet again to Anselm's criticism of Boso: "You have not yet weighed the gravity of sin."[2]

The second point I would like to raise concerns the concept of God. Though touched on only briefly in Professor Daly's discussion of foundations, this concept is central to the whole project of an environmental theology. To provide an adequate ecological theology, we need to rethink not only theological anthropology and its themes of creation, sin and grace, but also the basic idea of the divine in relation to the world. The symbol of God functions as the primary symbol of the whole religious system, the ultimate point of reference for understanding experience, life, and the world. The way in which a faith community shapes language about God implicitly represents what it takes to be the highest good, the profoundest truth, the most appealing beauty. Such speaking, in turn, powerfully molds the corporate identity of the community, shapes its worldview, and directs its praxis.

Professor Daly notes the distortion in the classical doctrine of God that emphasizes transcendence at the expense of immanence. Why was appreciation of God's immanence lost? Again patriarchy is a foundational reason. In classical theology, God is imagined on the model of the individual ruling male, in total control of all that happens, unrelated and unmoved by others as if such responsiveness would create dependency. God has no real relation to the world it is said, and the world remains outside of "Him" (the masculine pronoun is invariably used in patriarchal theology). Even when the Trinity is brought into the picture, attention remains with the Father and Son, the one generating, the other being begotten and sent to do the work of redemption.

An ecological theology needs to move away from this monarchical model and reconceive God in other ways: in mutual, if asymmetrical, relation to the universe, filled with passionate care for all creatures. Sallie McFague's excellent thought experiment about God as mother, lover, and friend of the world that is God's body is one way of reimagining God that awakens an ethic of responsibility and care. So, too, are the trinitarian theologies proposed by Jürgen Moltmann, Walter Kasper, Leonardo Boff, and Catherine LaCugna among others.[3] While open to criticism on various points, trinitarian theologies bring to the fore a crucial element that Professor Daly omits, namely, a view of ultimate reality as communion, with distinct persons nevertheless intrinsically related in a mutual dance of life (*perichoresis*).

Other ways of rethinking the doctrine of God are also possible. Western theology is notorious for neglect of the Holy Spirit. Pneumatology has even been called the "Cinderella" of theology.[4] And yet the Spirit is confessed in creed and psalms as the life-giver (*vivificantem*). She keeps on renewing the face of the earth as well as suffering persons and ravaged societies. She is God's indwelling presence at the heart of the world, building up bonds of connectedness.

A particular affinity exists between the Spirit, *Creator Spiritus*, and the natural world, not only in the beginning but throughout time. In the words of the fourteenth-century mystic and theologian Hildegaard of Bingen, the Spirit says:

> I, the highest and fiery power, have kindled every living spark and I have breathed out every breath of life. . . . I flame above the beauty of the fields; I shine in the waters; in the sun, the moon and the stars, I burn. And by means of the airy wind, I stir everything into quickness with a certain invisible life which sustains all. . . . I, the fiery power, lie hidden in these things and they blaze from me.[5]

Whirling everywhere like the wind the Spirit is God drawing near and passing by in vivifying, sustaining, renewing, and liberating power in the midst of cosmic and historical struggle. So profoundly is this true that whenever we speak in a generic way of "God," of the experience of God, or of God's doing something in the world, more often than not we are referring to the Spirit.

It is virtually impossible to imagine an unrelated, unmoved, or unilaterally transcendent Holy Spirit. Rethinking the mystery of God on the model of trinitarian communion in mutual relationship with the world, and remembering anew the vivifying Holy Spirit who dwells within all things and keeps on renewing the face of the earth, are essential tasks, I suggest, in grounding an ecological theology on a sure foundation, one that awakens people to their responsibility as partners with God's creative work.

As a third moment in this response I would like to raise four particular questions.

1. Appealing to the spirit of *noblesse oblige*, Professor Daly defends the uniqueness of human beings against those who would de-center humanity in the cosmos because of the arrogance that has come with a sense of humanity's higher powers. His defense is interestingly based on the notion that because humanity is a higher species we have a special responsibility to be proper stewards of the rest of creation. But both the attitude being critiqued (human domination over nature) and the attitude proposed in its place (responsible stewardship) operate within the same model, the pyramidal model of the hierarchy of being.

My question is this: would it not be more advantageous to break out of this model altogether? Granted it can operate in a beneficial way if human beings act responsibly. But it is a limited and limiting model in the face of the ecological crisis.

A more adequate model would take into account humanity's responsibility for the earth and our mutual interdependence on the earth for life and sustenance. For example, trees existed for millions of years before humans did. Their oxygen-making life process created the atmosphere, making it possible for humanity to evolve. In terms of people and trees, who needs whom more? Naturally speaking, the trees do not need our stewardship. They were fine before we arrived. Now we are cutting them down at a too-rapid rate which makes the responsible steward idea valuable. But this notion does not reveal the fundamental reality that humanity and all creatures inhabit this blue planet together and are mutually interrelated in a community of life. Yes, human beings have special responsibilities, but we are also dependent on others. Would not a kinship model, rather than a pyramid, be more adequate?

2. In his rethinking Professor Daly makes good use of the categories of process theology and suggests that they may be most adequate to our task. While I agree that this school of thought coheres with a contemporary scientific view of the world and has contributed much to our understanding, I ask whether Thomistic thought is not also a resource that Catholic theology, in particular, could tap.

The analogy of being, for example, is more than just an epistemological stratagem. It is an ontological category that expresses the relation of all things in the world to God by means of the notion of participation. Everything that exists does so through participation in divine being given to each as its own discrete finite act of existence. Everything participates in the incomprehensible liveliness of the living God. God is the wellspring of sheer aliveness whose act of being overflows, bringing the universe into existence and empowering it to be. This notion carries the companion recognition that all things are on fire with existence by participation in God's holy being which is unquenchable.[6] Divine transcendence and immanence are on equal footing here, rather than each being promoted at the expense of the other.

Similarly, the distinction between primary and secondary causality has great usefulness in orienting human action toward responsibility. Rather than leave us stymied by the "insoluble mode of God's action in the world," the notion of divine primary causality awakens the realization that God works in the world always and everywhere through secondary causes, through empowering the creature to acts of creation and self-transcendence. Evolution can be interpreted through this filter, so can the need for human responsibility; if we do not do it, it will not get done. Once again the immanence of divine action within human action comes to the fore. And so my query on these and other points; does the Thomistic tradition not have more to offer?

3. Should not eschatology be added to the areas of systematic theology that are open to development in the light of a renewed creation theology? Whether we understand echatology as an otherworldly end of things, a this-worldly reign of shalom, or a mystery of fulfillment that operates as a critical principle here and now, this doctrine is intrinsically relevant to creation. Without its perspective, thought about creation falls short of its goal.

4. The quotations from Karl Rahner cited by Professor Daly place the former squarely in the camp of those who have contributed to the anthropocentric theology that is now open to critique. Is there not something more positive to say about Rahner's contribution to our task? It was in his work that I, and I suspect many of my generation, first discovered the idea of a non-competitive relationship between God and the world (creatures develop in direct and not inverse proportion to their nearness to God). Rahner's monograph on hominisation traces evolution as the process of the self-transcendence of creatures made possible by the creative power of God intrinsic to them; his essay on christology and evolution connects Christian doctrine with the development of the earth at every stage.[7] As with feminism and Aquinas, are there not insights in Rahner that deserves a more hospitable hearing?

As a fourth point in this response, I would like to make a concrete suggestion. Given the power of symbol and prayer, I call on the Christian community to celebrate creation with a liturgical feast. Such a day could be called Creation Sunday; readings could be taken from Genesis 1 (six days of creation), Romans 8 (creation groaning), and Matthew 6 (Jesus' discourse about the lilies of the field), among other possibilities. Preaching could focus attention on theological and sacramental aspects of the earth as God's good creation and on humanity's delight and ethical responsibility as a unique part of the whole. Such a feast would not necessarily be an "issues" feast, which liturgists would rightly reject. Rather, it would be a God-centered celebration of divine creative power, of the universe arising from it, and of humanity's place within it. Such a day, I suggest, would contribute to care for the earth as a living creation with its own intrinsic worth and lift up the profound religious significance of this issue.

The second-century bishop Irenaeus penned a marvelous line. *"Gloria Dei vivens homo*: the glory of God is the human being fully alive."[8] In a Christian perspective converted from patriarchy, conscious of the integrity of creation, of the cosmic aspect of Christ's incarnation and redemption, and of the vivifying power of the Holy Spirit, we will be able to give this saying an ecological gloss: *gloria Dei vivens terra*: the glory of God is planet Earth, fully alive. Thus, may Christians be empowered to make our contribution to a worldwide ethic of responsibility and care.

NOTES

1. See Carolyn Merchant, *The Death of Nature: Women, Ecology, and the Scientific Revolution* (San Francisco: Harper and Row, 1980); Rosemary Radford Ruether, *New Woman, New Earth* (New York: Seabury, 1975); and Elizabeth Johnson. *Women, Earth, and Creator Spirit* (New York: Paulist, 1993).

2. Anselm of Canterbury. *Cur Deus Homo?* Book 1, Chapter 21.

3. Sallie McFague, *Models of God: Theology for an Ecological, Nuclear Age* (Philadelphia: Fortress, 1987); Jürgen Moltmann, *God in Creation* (San Francisco: Harper and Row, 1985); Walter Kasper, *The God of Jesus Christ* (New York: Crossroad, 1984); Leonardo Boff. *Trinity and Society* (Maryknoll, NY: Orbis, 1988); Catherine LaCugna, *God for Us: The Trinity and Christian Life* (San Francisco: Harper and Row, 1991); and Elizabeth Johnson, *She Who Is: The Mystery of God in Feminist Theological Discourse* (New York: Crossroad, 1992).

4. G.J. Sirks, "The Cinderella of Theology: The Doctrine of the Holy Spirit," *Harvard Theological Review* 50: 77–89.

5. From *Hildegaard of Bingen: Mystical Writings*. trans. Robert Carver and ed. Fiona Bowie and Oliver Davies (New York: Crossroad, 1990), 91–93.

6. See the fire metaphor for existence in Aquinas, *Summa Theologiae* I.8.a1.2.3.

7. Karl Rahner, *Hominisation: The Evolutionary Origin of Man as a Theological Problem* (New York: Herder & Herder, 1968), and his "Christology Within an Evolutionary View of the World, in *Theological Investigations* 5 (New York: Seabury, 1975), 157–92.

8. Irenaeus, *Adversus Haereses* 4.20.7 and 3.20.2.

Kevin W. Irwin

The Sacramentality of Creation and the Role of Creation in Liturgy and Sacraments

My purpose in this essay is to articulate some theological issues that lie at the heart of liturgical and sacramental celebration regarding the sacramentality of creation and the use of creation in worship. I will deal with (1) liturgical theology in general; (2) the interrelatedness of liturgy, sacraments, creation, and human life; (3) how creation is used in the liturgy since Vatican II; (4) the contemporary convergence between liturgical and creation theology; and (5) some critique of the liturgy regarding creation. The argument throughout is, in the main, from within the Roman Catholic tradition.

LITURGICAL THEOLOGY

The phrase *legem credendi lex statuat supplicandi*,[1] dated between 435–442 and generally ascribed to Prosper of Aquitaine,[2] has become something of a theme statement for many contemporary liturgists and sacramental theologians in their search for a method to articulate the theological meaning of the liturgy and the theology of liturgical enactment.[3]

While there is no agreed upon meaning for "liturgical theology" two general meanings are operative in contemporary writing.[4] First, liturgical theology is considered to be a reflection on the church's act of worship that draws out and explores in catechesis and systematic theology (particularly sacramental theology) the theological meaning of the liturgy: the actualization of the paschal mystery for the believing church through an act of proclaiming and hearing the Word and celebrating sacramental rituals. Second, liturgical theology is the use of liturgy as a source for systematic theology in the sense that terms and concepts operate theologically in liturgy; for example, God, Christ, Spirit, redemption, salvation, and sanctification can be probed for their theological meaning as derived from their use in liturgy.

The uniqueness of liturgy as fundamentally a *ritual action* is clearly understood and respected here with the result that the texts of the liturgy are not regarded as equivalent to other sources of positive theology (e.g., scripture, magisterium). Liturgical texts accompany symbolic actions and ritual gestures and it is only through taking these elements together that theological and spiritual meanings are disclosed. The fact that the church celebrates liturgy in order to experience the paschal mystery in a ritual event suggests both how important liturgy is as a source for theology and also the difficulty in delineating an acceptable method for engaging in liturgical theology.

More recently many liturgists and sacramental theologians[5] have argued in favor of expanding the *lex orandi, lex credendi* equation to include *lex agendi* so that the method of liturgical theology would include a critique of the present revised liturgy in light of liturgical tradition and contemporary needs. At present at least two meanings of *agendi* are commonly emphasized.

Actual Celebrations as a Theological Source

A number of contemporary proposals for liturgical method address the phenomenon of liturgy as *enacted* rites. These proposals point to the importance of using enacted liturgical rites as sources, *orandi*, from which to determine the church's belief, *credendi*. Thus, contemporary emphasis on *liturgy as event* sets the framework for developing a method in liturgical theology that deals with more than texts and with the texts themselves in the context of the liturgical action.[6] Such an investigation would consider how effectively the scriptures are proclaimed, prayed over, and preached, and how effectively they lead to the rest of the ritual, including the sacramental action that occurs through using elements from creation and euchological texts. This investigation would also consider to what extent symbolic interaction has been realized in the liturgy and to what extent the maximizing of symbolic engagement, as expressed in the general instructions (*praenotandae*) that accompany the rites as presently revised, does in fact occur.[7] For example, this investigation would call for asking whether baptism by immersion rather than infusion occurs commonly.

Another factor adding to the rationale of why a new method for engaging in liturgical theology is necessary is the nature of the present reform of the liturgy in Roman Catholicism and in other Christian churches which include the variety and flexibility of rites and texts within a ritual structure and the necessity of adapting, accommodating, and inculturating even this reformed liturgy.[8] On one level the variety possible in the reformed liturgy concerns *how* the liturgy is prepared and actually celebrated. The next level (of particular interest here) concerns how the celebration of the reformed liturgy is used as the source for liturgical theology developed from such varied rites. Attention moves beyond the texts found in ceremonial books to the shape and components of actual liturgical celebration where celebration provides the requisite context within which to interpret liturgical texts, symbolic actions, and ritual gestures.[9]

In addition to asking the question of "what is experienced" in actual liturgical rites, most liturgists who study the contemporary rites also inquire whether what is offered in the revised liturgy reflects the faith vision enunciated at Vatican II. The question pertains also to subsequent church documents calling for and shaping the reform of the liturgy as well as to the general instructions that accompany the revised rituals.[10] Thus the corollary of using actual celebrations as a theological source is evaluating the adequacy of liturgical celebrations in terms of what is said and enacted liturgically. This aspect of contemporary liturgical study is often termed the "critical function" of liturgical theology.[11]

Liturgy and Ethics

This second meaning of *lex agendi* concerns carrying out in life the implications of liturgical participation, a relationship that has traditionally been understood to constitute the act of worship. It recalls the work of pioneers in the liturgical movement who argued for an appreciation of liturgy that concerned the renewal of the church's whole life and the spiritual lives of those who participate.[12]

In this understanding, liturgical theology also addresses how what occurs in liturgy is reflected in the lives of its participants. The *lex orandi, lex credendi* axiom also gives attention to the *lex agendi* beyond actual celebration to what is sometimes called the *lex vivendi*[13]—how what is celebrated and believed is reflected in how the church lives its faith. Thus, the two foci of *lex orandi* and *lex credendi* yield a third element to the equation: *lex vivendi*, the life relation of the liturgy.[14]

Our argument deriving theological meanings from *enacted* rites means paying attention to creation as cited in liturgical texts, to how creation offers motives for praising God, to how creation itself is a demonstration of the divine in human life. It means attending to how the present reformed liturgy reflects a positive regard for the things of this earth simply because they are used in worship. The *vivendi* aspect of contemporary liturgical method can locate our inquiry into ecological awareness and concern as not only germane to liturgical theology but also concomitant with celebrating liturgy.

LITURGY, SACRAMENTS, CREATION, AND HUMAN LIFE

Among the underlying philosophical presuppositions and theological principles for considering liturgy as a privileged source for creation theology is the anthropological aptness[15] of liturgical and sacramental acts in terms of their constitutive elements. The use in worship of speech, gesture, elements of nature, and symbols that are the result of human manufacture is most fitting because these constitutive aspects of worship draw on commonly accepted aspects of human life, things from creation used in daily experience or actions regularly performed in life. For example, the use of water in baptism builds on the act of bathing, the use of bread and wine in the eucharist presumes the act of dining, the use of oil in the anointing of the sick supposes the human act of salving one's skin. In other words these "daily and domestic things" in human life, to use David Power's term, are the anthropological substratum for the liturgical/sacramental event.[16]

Some distinctions need to be made concerning the constitutive elements of liturgy and sacraments, for example, between words and symbols. On one level, one may cautiously distinguish words from symbols because words are the means of verbal communication and symbols are the means of nonverbal interaction; yet, on another level as we will soon see, words themselves are symbols. A further distinction can be made between symbols that are derived from nature (e.g., water) and symbols that are the result of human productivity (e.g., bread and wine). That liturgy uses words and symbols together in a repertoire of ritual activity is to acknowledge the anthropological rootedness of worship in human life and particularly in human behavior. The joint use of words and symbols in worship is respectful of the human person and the means humans use for communication and interaction.

In this connection, Louis Marie Chauvet argues for a symbolic understanding of both word and creation as used in worship.[17] If the literal meaning of the Greek term *symballein* is "to throw together" and the noun form is "that which is thrown together," then the liturgy of the Word at its most profound level is "symbolic." The liturgy of the Word is a "symbolic rehearsal of salvation" in the sense that the repeated hearing and appropriation of the Word implies the requisite response of the faith assembly. The literal meaning of the Greek verb implies that symbols require a response from one already in a relationship of shared meaning; in liturgy, shared faith. The purpose of the scriptural word is to place in relationship, to encounter the other, to reunite that which ought to be understood together. One can argue then that the notion of "symbolic language" is redundant in the sense that the word as a medium for communication implies a speaking to and a response by those addressed. What is offered in the symbolic word requires a response of acceptance, encounter, and appropriation. Similarly symbols from material creation are themselves elements that by their nature require a response by the believing community.

What is central here is the *use* of symbols taken from creation and the *symbolic engagement* in worship made possible by the use of creation. Such engagement is opposed to objectification of symbols or their reduction to being signs since both objectification and signs most usually convey *one* meaning and have a one-to-one correspondence with what they signify. On the other hand the polyvalent meanings intrinsically attached to symbolic engagement are all unleashed in liturgy by the very fact that elements from creation and symbolic actions are used. These meanings can be either positive or negative.[18] In sacramental celebration, some of these meanings are articulated verbally in the blessing prayers that accompany symbolic usage. The theological value of euchology (i.e., blessing prayers, especially the eucharistic prayer and other presidential prayers). Generally these significations are derived from salvation history wherein these events are paradigmatic and applicable in the present through the experience of liturgy. These meanings from salvation history most often articulate obvious positive meanings; sometimes they give a positive dimension to what would otherwise be understood as negative.[19] The variety of meanings present in such texts, when appropriated into a liturgical theology of what is celebrated, gives direction to the polyvalent meanings inherent in the use of symbols.

In addition, the liturgical use of symbols from creation has the effect of expressing what is really inexpressible—that liturgy draws us into an ever deepening relationship with God in the manifold ways that salvation can be understood and reflected in liturgical prayer texts. Thus, the use of water in initiation is meant to evoke its pluriform meanings through the act of washing; the act draws those bathed in water into a relationship with God, through Christ's paschal mystery in the power of the Spirit enacted in the church.

Furthermore, the use of symbols that result from human productivity, for example, bread and wine, point to the theological meaning of the use of elements from creation that require human ingenuity for their manufacture. The classical argument that bread and wine are constitutive of the eucharist suggests (at least on one level) that human intelligence and ingenuity also form part of the reality of the liturgy. This example implies and underscores the importance of the agrarian cycle of planting and harvesting and the acts of refining wheat into grains, mixing ingredients for the dough (including "destroying" the grains to make the dough and the dough rising, usually twice before baking) and baking that signify that human work is necessary for the eucharist to take place. This prizing of human productivity also conveys the theological value of the work. "No work, no worship." In current debate, however, bread and wine are not regarded as necessarily constitutive. Arguments in favor of "staple food" and "festive drink" replace the convenient "bread and wine" couplet in some discussions. Such an adjustment to alternate foods should not, however, diminish the value of our argument about human ingenuity and productivity, in particular the cycles of nature and agrarian "dying and rising."[20]

The fact that liturgy rests on symbolic words and a symbolic use of created elements from human life, articulates for Christians that God is discoverable in human life and that the encounter with God in liturgy derives from and returns to this human life. One of the purposes of the graced events of liturgy and sacraments is to experience Christ's mediation of salvation to the believing church. This mediation occurs through the power of the Spirit in ritual actions that derive from the incarnational principle that the Christian God is experienced in all life through the eyes of faith (for example, in seven sacraments, in praying the liturgy of the hours, in rites of profession and burial).

One of the purposes of liturgy and sacraments is to articulate how God is experienced as savior in and through the liturgy and how this same God is discoverable and discovered in the rest of life. The patristic maxim *caro salutis est cardo* (the flesh is the instrument of salvation) grounds the act of liturgy as based on human means of communication and self-expression.[21] Put in more explicitly theological language, the principles of incarnation and mediation are articulated in the act of liturgy and the act of liturgy continues the mediation of salvation in explicit ways (again in seven sacraments, in praying the liturgy of the hours, in rites of profession and burial).

In our argument, priority is always given to symbolic engagement and liturgical participation through symbol as means used to draw the community to share more fully in the mystery of God, a communion that can be imaged in a number of ways and experienced through the use of symbol. The objectification of given symbolic elements used in liturgy, for example, bread and wine for the eucharist, can paradoxically diminish the reality of the symbols on which sacramental liturgy and liturgical theology are based for at least two reasons.

First, because symbolic elements complement the symbolic word as essentially dialogic realities, to emphasize symbols as objects reduces, for example, the essentially dialogic character of consecrated bread and wine as a specification of having shared in the proclaimed Word, which itself is inherently dialogical, and of Christ's paschal mystery as presented in the texts of the preface and eucharistic prayer. The act of communion signifies the ratification on the human's part of the offer of Christ through these symbolic means. Bread and wine are consecrated to be eaten and drunk by those who participate. This traditional tenet of Roman Catholic theology and practice is in the canons of the Council of Trent which note that the eucharist, by its nature, is "to be received" (ut sumatur [cf. Matthew 26, 26ss] insitiutum, DS 1643). "To put it another way: the first truth of the eucharistic doctrine is, 'this is my body,' not 'here I am present'."[22]

Second, because the presumed ecclesial community for whom symbols function in liturgy is often left out of a theology based on objectified symbols, such as real presence, there is a diminished ecclesiological aspect to eucharistic theology that is all the more jarring since the eucharistic prayers that have been added to the Roman Rite in the present reform all contain explicit epicleses about drawing the church community into deeper unity. These prayers are legitimately used to illustrate the traditional (often termed "Augustinian") emphasis placed on church unity as deepened through eucharistic sharing and as specified in euchological texts, the prayers over the gifts, and prayers after communion.[23] That the text of 1 Corinthians 11:23–32 about the one bread signifying church unity is based on the image of one loaf being shared by all is a significant illustration of the range of meanings that can be derived from the use of creation and symbol in worship. Most fitting is the way the prayer in the *Didache* 9:4 elaborates on the symbolic meaning of broken bread when it refers to the process of human ingenuity involved in how bread is manufactured: "As this broken bread was scattered over the mountains, and when brought together became one, so let your Church be brought together from the ends of the earth into your kingdom."[24]

Thus, in our understanding the operative notion of symbol in the liturgy is dynamic; it involves and ultimately transforms the community. Consequently, the liturgical theology derived from symbols used in the context of the liturgy simply cannot concern "objects" alone. Nor can it refer to symbols, especially those from creation, simply as a means to an experience of God. To use creation in liturgy is to show reverence for creation through, with, and in which the incarnate God is disclosed and discovered. The use of material creation in the liturgy has traditionally been understood to reflect back to the creator and to imply an understanding that rests on the sound foundation of theological anthropology.[25] The use of creation in the liturgy overcomes the problem of the spiritual/material dualism sometimes found in theology.[26]

In the case of the theological anthropology of liturgy and sacraments, representative Roman Catholic thought in a similar vein asserts:

A sacrament is not a stand-in for something else, a visible sign for some other invisible reality. The essence of a sacrament is the capacity to reveal grace, the agapic self-gift of God, by being what it is. By being thoroughly itself, a sacrament bodies forth the absolute self-donative love of God that undergirds both it and the entirety of creation. By its nature a sacrament requires that it be appreciated for what it is and not as a tool to an end; in Buber's terms, a sacrament is always "thou."[27]

Thus part of the anthropological and theological foundation upon which the act of liturgy is based is the use of creation and symbolic interaction through which means the divine is disclosed and faith in the divine is shaped and renewed in the church. If one of the purposes of liturgy and sacraments is to give voice and expression to the inarticulate but real praise of God in creation by the very use of creation in worship, it is the purpose of the next two sections of this paper to articulate some of the ways in which the present revised liturgy does this. *Lex orandi* will be used to indicate directions for a *lex credendi*, wherein the role of creation in liturgy and sacraments is emphasized, and of *lex vivendi* about living out in all of life what was celebrated in the liturgy.

CONTEMPORARY LEX ORANDI: HOW CREATION IS USED

Times for Celebration

The determination of times for celebration[28] of the daily liturgy of the hours, the seasons of the church year and some feast days derive from the rhythm of the cosmos. The determination of dawn for morning prayer and dusk for evening prayer is underscored in the General Instruction on the Hours which states that morning prayer is "celebrated . . . as the light of a new day is dawning" (n. 38). It is appropriate that Zechariah's canticle is always used at this hour:

> *The dawn from on high shall break upon us,*
> *to shine on those who dwell in darkness*
> *and the shadow of death . . . (Luke 1:79).*

It is not a coincidence that this same text is used as the communion antiphon for the Solemnity of the Birth of John the Baptist since the date of this feast, June 24, was deliberately chosen in accord with the length of the sun's rays as experienced in the northern hemisphere.[29] Just as the daylight begins to diminish after June 21 (often called "the longest day of the year") the church commemorates the birth of the Baptist whose saying "Jesus must increase, but I must decrease" (John

3:30) determined the date for this commemoration. The sign of diminishing daylight in the cosmos has determined the feast of the one whose self-effacement ("decrease") led to people's putting their faith in Christ ("the dawn from on high"). That this feast has a rich tradition of liturgical importance is attested to by the fact that the only other births commemorated in the calendar are those of Jesus and the Blessed Virgin Mary. Its significance is further emphasized by the number of Mass formulas honoring the Baptist in the (very early) Verona collection of euchology.[30] In the present Sacramentary, moreover, the only saints who have their own preface besides John the Baptist are the Blessed Virgin Mary, St. Joseph (March 19), and Saints Peter and Paul (June 29).

> With regard to evening prayer the same Instruction states that when evening approaches and the day is already far spent, evening prayer is celebrated . . . [when] we join the Churches of the East in calling upon the "joy-giving light of holy glory" . . . [and we sing in praise] now that we have come to the setting of the sun and seen the evening star (n. 39).

The Jewish tradition of the *lucernarium*, the lighting of the lamps in the Temple at evening prayer, is also part of the liturgical ritual traditionally attached to this hour.[31]

The phases of the moon and its location determine the date for our celebration of Easter.[32] The diminishing of the intensity of the sun in the northern hemisphere is reflected in the lectionary and euchology of Advent and Christmas, which texts become the more compelling when this natural phenomenon is recalled and experienced. Part of the Johannine Prologue, the traditional gospel on Christmas morning, states that "The light shines on in darkness a darkness that did not overcome it (John 1:5).[33] The following euchological texts now used at Christmas and Epiphany are the more notable when their cosmic context is recalled.

Father,
you make this holy night radiant
with the splendor of Jesus Christ
our light (opening prayer, Mass at Midnight).[34]

Father,
we are filled with new light
by the coming of your Word among us
(opening prayer, Mass at Dawn).[35]

In the wonder of the incarnation your eternal Word has brought to the eyes of faith a new and radiant vision of your glory (Christmas preface I).[36]

Today in him a new light has dawned upon the world (Christmas preface III).[37]

Today you revealed in Christ your eternal plan of salvation and showed him as the light of all peoples (Epiphany preface).[38]

The addition of the Isaiah 9:1–6 ("A people who walked in darkness have seen a great light") to the traditional scripture readings for Midnight Mass (Titus 2:11–14 and Luke 2:10–11) also underscores the light symbolism of Christmas.

It is commonly asserted that a preexisting (pagan) feast of ingathering the first fruits of the Fall harvest influenced Judaism's practice of celebrating *sukkoth* ("tabernacles" or "booths") as a Fall festival of covenant renewal.[39] This same idea is congenial in Christianity with celebrations commemorating the "first fruits of creation" in the apocalyptic and eschatological themes reflected in the Lectionary for Mass prior to and on the First Sunday of Advent. The second reading on the Last Sunday of the Year "B" cycle (the Solemnity of Christ the King) contains the text, "Jesus Christ is the faithful witness, the first-born from the dead and ruler of the kings of earth" (Revelation 1:5).[40]

That the Johannine prologue (read on Christmas day) uses a variation on the word "booths" or "tabernacles" is also significant; it acclaims that "the Word . . . made his dwelling among us" (John 1:14). The verb form in Greek is literally "he set up his tent" or "he tabernacled" among us. (Though it is not part of the historical rationale that lead to the commemoration of All Saints and All Souls at this time of year, our present celebration of All Saints and All Souls is connected with the theme of "first fruits of creation.")

Motivation for Celebration

Praise to God the creator[41] is constitutive of the theology of the liturgy of the hours. For example, a hymn of praise for the days of creation was assigned to ferial vespers for each day (except first vespers of Sunday) in the former breviary.[42] This usage is retained in the *editio typica* of the present revision. These texts, probably from the same author (some would say Gregory the Great), devote four stanzas to the work of each day of creation. Sunday's vesper hymn, *Lucis creator optime*, which reflects the light and darkness motif of evening prayer, begins with the following verses:

O blest Creator of the light,
Who mak'st the day with radiance bright,
And o'er the forming world didst call
The light from chaos first of all;
Whose wisdom joined in meet array
The more and eve, and named them Day:
Night comes with all its darkling fears;
Regard thy people's prayers and tears.[43]

The rest of the vesper hymns reflecting praise for the days of creation are *Immense coeli conditor*, "O great Creator of the sky" (Monday);[44] *Telluris alme conditor*, "Earth's mighty maker, whose command/ Raised from the sea the solid land" (Tuesday); *Caeli Deus sanctissime*, "O God whose hand hath spread the sky, And all its shining hosts on high" (Wednesday); *Magnae Deus potentiae*, "O Sovereign Lord of nature's might, Who bad'st the water's birth divide; Part in the heavens to take their flight, And part in ocean's deep to hide" (Thursday); and *Hominis supernae conditor*, "Maker of man, who from Thy throne,/ Dost order all things, God alone" (Friday). The hymn for first vespers of Sunday, *Iam sol recedit igneus*, by a different author (perhaps St. Ambrose), moves from the days of creation to praising the Trinity[45] in the morning and evening.[46]

What makes the retention of these hymns in the *editio typica* of the revised breviary of particular note is that in the present structure for evening prayer the third "psalm" is actually a christological hymn from the New Testament, two of which deal specifically with praise for creation. One could make a case for the appropriate juxtaposition at this hour of praise for the days of creation and for our re-creation in Christ. Because these hymns specify Christ in connection with praise for creation any "generic deism" associating the Christian God with creation is avoided. (More will be said below about these christological hymns.)

At Sunday morning prayer the use of the canticle from Daniel 3 (verses 56, and 57–88 are used Sunday week I and verses 52–57 are used Sunday weeks II and IV) is significant in this connection. The opening verse: "Bless the Lord, all you works of the Lord praise and exalt him above all forever . . . (57)" is followed by a series of acclamations citing various facets of creation and redemption as motives for praising God. These include verses about praise for creation[47] and praise for redemption[48] with praise for redemption ending the canticle.[49] These same motives for praising God are found in much of the psalter, and in the present arrangement of the hours "praise psalms" are used as the third psalm at morning prayer, many of which contain explicit praise of God for creation (e.g., Psalms 19, 29, 65, 147, 148, 150).[50]

That the liturgy of the hours classically begins with Psalm 94, paralleling the combined themes of praising God for creation and redemption is an additional illustration of acclaiming the God of creation.[51] Two phrases from the *Te Deum* (used at the conclusion of the office of readings on most Sundays and solemnities) capture and summarize this theology:

> All creation worships you. . . .
> Holy, holy, holy, Lord, God of power and might,
> heaven and earth are full of your glory.

Fittingly, these last two lines are repeated in the preface acclamation (*Sanctus*) in the present eucharistic prayers. These prayers praise God for the *mirabilia Dei*,[52] especially in creation and redemption; they are derived from the "blessing" (*berakah*) and "thanksgiving" (*todah*) traditions of Jewish prayer.[53]

> Appropriately, our song is a quotation from the seraphim who surround God's throne with fiery praise. While in the Jerusalem temple, Isaiah sees a vision of God's transcendent holiness, and the angels are singing "Holy, Holy, Holy Lord, God" (Isaiah 6:3). Again in the Apocalypse the creatures around the heavenly throne join the angels in chanting: "Holy, Holy, Holy is the Lord God Almighty" (Revelation 4:8). Both visions attest God's majesty. In Isaiah, all space, heaven and earth, is filled with God; in Revelation, all time—past, present and future—is filled with the Lord.[54]

This acclamation combines praise for creation with praise for redemption, and specifies the obedient life, death, and resurrection of Jesus. This combination of themes is part of the "classical" shape of eucharistic anaphoras,[55] even though this motif is all too briefly expressed.[56]

The theology operative in the fourth eucharistic prayer in the present Sacramentary concerns praising God who has made all things and who is the source of all life.[57] It brings out the universal need for the paschal mystery and the universal effects that flow from it.[58] The preface to this prayer refers to the entire creation and to the Father as the ultimate source of creation and the one who is manifested in creation. Human beings fulfill the purpose of creation in giving voice to creation's praise of God by joining in the praise that is voiced in liturgy,[59] in particular the eucharist. This prayer is a worldview in a capsule form.

> Because of the goodness of the Father, the Church joins in the hymn of the angels. All other creatures on earth are enabled to express their praise through the voices of those in the Church who speak for the mute creatures. Thus the praise takes on cosmic proportions.[60]

An important example of how praising God for creation functions as a motive for giving thanks, recounting the fall, and establishing why humankind needed a savior, is found in the *Apostolic Constitutions*, Book VIII.[61] Significantly, this prayer concerns praising God for creation, for sustaining in life all that God has created, for the history of salvation, and for sending Jesus as redeemer. Its christological section capitalizes on a number of paradoxes, notably the statement that he who was present at creation is now "the firstborn of all creation."

In the liturgy, the value of creation, as reflecting the power of God and as the arena in which divine salvation overturns universal estrangement from God, is exemplified by the selection of the first creation account, Genesis 1:1–2:2, as the first reading at the Easter Vigil.[62] The recounting of this text, which is allied with other such texts called "cosmogonic myths,"[63] praises God the creator, redeemer, and sustainer of all life.[64] It has special poignancy because it accompanies the annual recreation of the earth in the Spring. Its repetition reflects the belief that the act of creation is not simply what happened once in history but something eternally accomplished by God's creative word.[65] In fact, one could argue that this text really recounts what God intended in creation, not what really resulted, and that its annual proclamation at Easter facilitates an interpretation that creation happens among us through Christ even as we yearn for the "new heavens and a new earth." The texts of the prayers that follow this reading at the Easter vigil are significant:

> *Almighty and eternal God,*
> *you created all things in wonderful beauty and order.*
> *Help us now to perceive*
> *how still more wonderful is the new creation*

by which in the fullness of time
you redeemed your people
through the sacrifice of our passover, Jesus Christ. . . .[66]

Lord, God,
the creation of man was a wonderful work,
his redemption still more wonderful.
May we persevere in right reason
against all that entices to sin
and so attain to everlasting joy.[67]

At the very beginning of the (preface to the) Roman canon, the Roman liturgy has traditionally used the title, *Domine, sancte Pater, omnipotens et aeternae Deus,*[68] containing the three dominant names for God found in most contemporary prayers.[69] Fittingly, the last phrase of the preface contains the phrase (from Isaiah 6:3) and leads to naming God in the following way: *Sanctus, sanctus, sanctus Dominus Deus sabaoth. Pleni sunt caeli et terra gloria tua.*

The mediating function of creation is exemplified in a specifically *christological* sense in the liturgical use of such scripture texts as the Johannine prologue (John 1:1–14, used on Christmas day) and the christological hymn in the letter to the Colossians (1:15–20, specifically 15–18, used as one of the New Testament hymns at evening prayer). According to the Johannine prologue, God's creative idea is the Logos, the second divine person. The "high" christology of the preexistent Logos in the prologue combined with the introductory words of the prologue "in the beginning" (recalling the first words of Genesis proclaimed at the Easter vigil) underscore how Christ was present and active at the creation of the world. John 1:3 summarizes this idea: "through him all things came into being, and apart from him nothing came to be." The recreation of the world was accomplished through the same Christ, cited at the prologue's end as "the Word [who] became flesh, and made his dwelling among us, and we have seen his glory, filled with enduring love" (v. 14).

Similarly the Colossians hymn (1:12–20) emphasizes Christ's preexistence. The purpose of all creation consists in our union with Christ and through him with the Father, the origin and fulfillment of all creation, including humanity. Of particular note is verse 16: "In him everything in heaven and on earth was created, things visible and invisible . . . all things were created through him." Thus, we can assert that the stated motivation for liturgical praise is creation and redemption and that the dynamic of Christian liturgy is to offer back creation to the creator through Christ, the co-creator.[70]

This emphasis on the christological axis of liturgy, specifically the paschal mystery, has recently been appropriately supplemented by a pneumatologically rich emphasis on liturgy and sacraments as experiences through and in which the church is drawn into the life of the triune God. All liturgy is triune. It is the triune God who makes it occur. Just as Jürgen Moltmann can rightly argue that creation is the result of the power and life of the Spirit, thus ending what perhaps can be regarded as too christological an approach to creation, so we can emphasize that the liturgy is dependent on the dynamism of the Trinity (particularly when understood both immanently and economically).[71]

The renewed emphasis on the theological meaning of the epiclesis in the eucharistic anaphoras added to the Roman rite in the present reform and in all other blessing prayers (e.g., to bless water at initiation) gives added stimulus to the theological elaboration of the role of the Trinity, and particularly of the Spirit, in all liturgy. It is the triune God who gathers the assembly into the praying church, that is "the family you have gathered here before you."[72] In addition to the use of the indicative mood in verbs in the anaphora, the use of the subjunctive characterizes the epiclesis. When the text of the second eucharistic prayer reads:

> Let your Spirit come upon these gifts to make them holy,
> so that they may become for us
> the body and blood of our Lord, Jesus Christ. . . .
> May all of us who share in the body and blood of Christ
> be brought together in the unity of the Holy Spirit.[73]

The *lex orandi* of the Roman rite overcomes the weakness of the lack of an explicit epiclesis in the Roman canon and draws on a wider euchological tradition to substantiate the addition of such texts that explicitly invoke the Spirit with the deferential verb form of the subjunctive.[74] Such usages illustrate the central importance of understanding liturgy as initiated by, sustained in, and reaching its perfection through the Trinity.

Explicit faith in the Trinity is also illustrated in the creed:[75]

> Credo in unum Deum,
> Patrem omnipotentem, factorem caeli et terrae
> visibilium omnium et invisibilium
> Et in unum Dominum Iesum Christum . . .

per quem omnia facta sunt. . . .
Et in Spiritum Sanctum, Dominum et vivificantem.

Thus, the act of creation is not limited to the Father; it is equally christological and pneumatological.[76]

That the Christian church has traditionally used the doxology to
end the psalms at the hours and now also uses it to end the New Testament hymns at evening prayer[77] is another explicit attestation of the
role of the Trinity in the liturgy. When the doxology is added to Psalm
94 a happy coincidence of praising the triune God for creation occurs.
The text of the original doxology: "Glory to the Father, through the Son
in the (unity of the) Holy Spirit . . ." is especially applicable because of
its connotation of the church being drawn into and abiding in the Trinity.

Water, the Use of Symbols

The methodological concern in this section is merely to illustrate the
importance of the use of symbols in liturgy as derived from the general
instruction of a given rite and from the liturgical ritual itself. The specific example chosen is *water* as described and used in the present Rite
of the Christian Initiation of Adults (hereafter RCIA).[78]

Symbolic Use: The general instruction on Christian initiation states
that "The water used in baptism should be true water and, both for the
sake of authentic sacramental symbolism and for hygienic reasons, [it]
should be pure and clean" (n. 8).[79] "The baptismal font . . . should be
spotlessly clean and of pleasing design" (n. 9). These texts overturn
centuries of usage (from Trent on) when the baptismal water blessed at
the Easter vigil was stored in baptisteries to be used for a whole year.
Water's freshness and life-giving properties are underscored in this
rubrical change. Now the water blessed at Easter is used only during
the Easter season in which case a "thanksgiving" prayer for water
already blessed is used. The instruction goes on to explain how the
water will be used in the act of water baptism: "either immersion,
which is more suitable as a symbol of participation in the death and
resurrection of Christ, or pouring may lawfully be used" (n. 22). Thus,
the water blessing leads to water being used in the baptismal bathing
with water.

The rite for adult initiation offers three texts for blessing the water
and two for offering thanksgiving for the blessed water. The rubrics for
the first of these prayers state that toward the end of the prayer (after
recounting a host of images about the use of water in salvation
history), the celebrant "touches the water with his right hand." This

simple rubric suggests that the freshness and life-giving properties of water are to be emphasized by hearing and seeing the water move, thus becoming "living" water. The text that accompanies this gesture derives from Romans 6:3–11, and the correlation is particularly important when this passage and blessing are used together at the Easter vigil:

> *We ask you, Father, with your Son*
> *to send the Holy Spirit upon the waters of this font.*
> *May all who are buried with Christ in the death of baptism*
> *rise also with him to newness of life.*
> *We ask this. . . . (222 A)*

The rite for adult initiation also states that the celebration of baptism takes place at "the baptismal font, if this is in view of the faithful; otherwise in the sanctuary, where a vessel of water for the rite should be prepared beforehand" (218). These explicit directions indicate the value of communal participation in the use of water in the liturgy of baptism. That pluriform meanings belong to the liturgical use of symbol is exemplified in the following discussion of water as used in the rite of adult initiation.

Theological Meanings

The rubrics to the RCIA state that "water is God's creation," and immediately describe the "sacramental use of water" as important for the "unfolding of the paschal mystery" in water baptism and in remembering "God's wonderful works in the history of salvation" (210). Then the RCIA invokes "the Holy Trinity at the very outset of the celebration of baptism" calling to "mind the mystery of God's love from the beginning of the world and the creation of the human race."

> By invoking the Holy Spirit and proclaiming Christ's death and resurrection, [the use of water] impresses on the mind the newness of Christian baptism, by which we share in his own death and resurrection and receive the holiness of God (210).

The importance of water is cited in the introduction to the Litany of the Saints: "May [God] give them the new life of the Holy Spirit, whom we are about to call down on this water" (220). In both thanksgiving prayers the term "consecrated water" is used to designate the effects to be derived from it:

By the mystery of this consecrated water lead them to a new and spiritual birth (222 D,E).

The act of baptizing in water is described in no fewer than five places as *washing*. The rite states clearly that

the celebration of baptism has as its center and highpoint the baptismal washing and the invocation of the Holy Trinity. Beforehand there are rites that have an inherent relationship to the baptismal washing (209).

At the conclusion of the preparatory rites on Holy Saturday the final blessing of the elect draws on the example of the "holy prophets" who proclaimed to all who would draw near to God "wash and be cleansed." The result of this act is "rebirth in the Spirit," being "reborn as [God's] children" and entering "the community of [God's] Church" (203). During the rite, immediately after the profession of faith, the elect receive Christ's paschal mystery "as expressed in the washing with water" (212). The rubrics state that

The washing with water should take on its full importance as the sign of that mystical sharing in Christ's death and resurrection through which those who believe in his name die to sin and rise to eternal life (212).

It then places immersion before infusion as the way to administer the baptismal washing (as stated also in 226), which usages are not a mere "purification rite but the sacrament of being joined to Christ" (213).[80]

The allied notion of baptismal *cleansing* also finds a prominent place in four of the blessing prayers. In one God is praised for having "created water to cleanse and give life" (222 B). Three others end with the same phrase:

You have called your children . . . to this cleansing water and new birth (222 C,D,E).

In addition, both options for the exorcism to be prayed over the elect at the first scrutiny capitalize on the gospel story of the Samaritan woman (John 4:5–42) proclaimed that day,[81] and the prayer over the elect at the presentation of the Lord's Prayer adapts the "living water."[82]

The scriptural allusion to Jesus' crucifixion in John 19:34, "and immediately blood and water poured out" (and at least indirectly 1

John 5:8: ". . . there are three witnesses, the Spirit, the water, and the blood . . ."[83]), is incorporated in two of the three blessing prayers for water and in one of the two thanksgiving prayers for water already blessed.[84] It is also used in the prayer accompanying the anointing after baptism when confirmation is separated from baptism.[85]

The description of the effects of the water used at baptism[86] is stated in the general instruction on Christian initiation: "This first sacrament pardons all our sins, rescues us from the power of darkness, and brings us to the dignity of adopted children, a new creation through water and the Holy Spirit" (n. 2).[87] The rite itself cites "life," "new life," "new birth," and "rebirth" resulting from baptism.[88]

It is clear from this methodological example about one aspect of the *lex orandi* for adult initiation that the revised rites offer a wealth of material from which to develop a liturgical theology of baptism. The value placed on creation is implicit throughout the rite, and the theological meaning of sharing in the paschal mystery is reiterated throughout and is particularly clear when water baptism is done by immersion. Thus, we have exemplified the crucial role that symbolic usage plays in the doing of sacraments and in theological reflection about church's *lex orandi*.

Bread and Wine

Manufactured Symbols: In addition to symbols from creation the liturgy uses symbols that result from the "work of human hands," among which are bread and wine, though I do not mean to ignore in my argument the indigenization issue concerning whether bread and wine ought not be replaced by other foods—making "substantial food and festive drink" a more suitable phase in this discussion.

Philippe Rouillard has argued that the institution of the eucharist during the course of a meal "is deeply rooted in a human action indispensable to life and . . . rich in human and sacred symbolism: eating and drinking and having a meal."[89] In so treating the "symbolism of bread and wine," Rouillard asserts that these "fundamental elements of the nourishment of people in the Mediterranean basin . . . are rich in symbolism"[90] and that their manufacture relies on the cycle of dying and rising in nature which most fittingly symbolizes the dying and rising of Jesus.

That these elements rely on the agrarian cycle (and the cosmic symbolism) of planting seeds, which then "die" in the earth and "rise" to become mature stalks of wheat and bunches of grapes, is most significant. At their harvesting, the plants "die" once again by being picked and are then crushed to produce the raw material of wheat flour and grape juice. Other ingredients are then added to the flour, especially yeast, to make a dough that rises (at least once) and which, after baking, becomes bread. The liquid derived from crushing the grapes is preserved in casks to age, to mature, and thus to become wine. These "produced" elements are then taken as the most apt symbols to commemorate the death and resurrection of Jesus in the eucharistic meal (at least as classically understood in Western Christianity). These elements of nourishment are then consecrated as the church's eucharistic food.

The aptness of the use of bread and wine points to the central, christological axis of the liturgy. A harmony between creation theology and the paschal mystery is disclosed here by the fact that the symbolism of using manufactured symbols at the eucharist sustains both creation and redemption. The key to interpreting these elements is human ingenuity and productivity. In other words, the cycle of dying and rising and the employing of the "work" of human labor are factors intrinsic to the eucharist and for the liturgical theology of the eucharist.[91]

Our interest in symbolic usage is borne out in the eucharistic species in two ways. First, the context for the celebration of the eucharist requires that cycles of nature and human manufacture together form the source for the eucharistic symbols. Second, the consecrated bread and wine are designated for use in the liturgy in such a way that breaking and sharing one bread and sharing one cup in the church assembly (as found in 1 Corinthians 11 and frequently repeated in patristic and subsequent descriptions of the eucharist)[92] is the focal point toward which consecration and transformation leads.

Pluriform Meanings: The use of the eucharist in various settings draws out different theological emphases. For example, the celebration of the eucharist as part of the Easter vigil is the clearest symbolic usage of the "first-fruits" of the new creation. The rubrics state that the eucharist is given only as viaticum on Holy Saturday and that the bread and wine to be used at the vigil are "brought forward by the newly baptized." Behind these rubrical guidelines is an understanding of the end of the "old leaven" (signifying our former way of life) and the beginning of the new leaven with new eucharistic breads (signifying new life in the risen Christ). This symbolism is sustained in one of the options for the second reading on Easter Sunday from 1 Corinthians 5:6–8 (part of which is the communion antiphon for the vigil, 1 Corinthians 5:7–8).

Other contexts for the celebration of the eucharist draw out other theological meanings. These include the motif of the renewal of the covenant of baptism since the cup-word at the institution narrative speaks about "the new and everlasting covenant." Sunday eucharist is particularly noteworthy in this regard when the rite of blessing and sprinkling with holy water is used. The eucharist as a rite of passage is clearly specified when the eucharist is given outside of Mass to the dying. The special prayers for the rite of administering viaticum are most helpful to draw out this somewhat neglected aspect of eucharistic theology.[93] The following instances are of special interest: the rubric that "the priest explains [in the homily] the meaning and importance of viaticum" (n. 189); an alternative to the customary invitation to communion, "Jesus Christ is the food for our journey; he calls us to the heavenly table"; and two prayers after communion that refer to the eucharist as a rite of passage, specifically of being led "safely into the kingdom of light" and of entering "your kingdom in peace" (n. 209).[94]

This explication of the church's *lex orandi* reflects our contention that liturgical rites taken as a whole (i.e., symbols, scripture, and euchological texts) disclose how the church's prayer both reveres and uses creation in its liturgical prayer.

CONVERGENCE: LITURGICAL AND CREATION THEOLOGY

This particular moment in history affords a unique opportunity to articulate important strands of convergence between liturgical studies and creation theology, the combination of which articulates theological depth and argues for the preservation of creation for the integrity and quality of liturgical and sacramental engagement. The present reform of the liturgy builds on the Roman rite's use and reverence for symbol and symbolic engagement and maximizes such engagement because it is precisely through these means that God is revealed and encountered.

The rubrical directives for greater use of elements from creation in worship[95] are faithful to the tradition of the Roman rite. They also transcend the minimalist approach to symbolic interaction in liturgy and sacraments that resulted from the rubrical precision and fixity of the Roman rite after Trent. This kind of theological statement substantiates the contemporary concern for the environment because the very act of liturgy is imperiled when creation is threatened. The foundations for reviving a theology of symbol for liturgy and sacrament are similarly imperiled because of the diminished quality of the earth's resources. Simultaneously, however, the rootedness of Christian liturgy in creation needs to be articulated all the more today so that liturgical and sacramental theology may be faithful to their anthropological roots and articulate a theology in harmony with the revised rites.

A creation-centered theology of liturgy would ground the liturgical act as anthropologically apt. A creation focus for liturgical theology would ground and express the trinitarian theology of worship by emphasizing how the Trinity was operative in creation and is operative in sustaining creation as an expression of God's nature and goodness. A creation focus for liturgical theology would offer the most appropriate category within which the value of aesthetics may be argued. Such an argument would emphasize that that which is aesthetically pleasing reflects the glory of God and that aesthetically pleasing arts and artifacts are intrinsic to the experience of liturgy and theology. As the categories of the good, the true, and the beautiful are being revived as crucial for contemporary ethics, so the theology developed from the reformed liturgy necessarily includes them and gives them shape.[96] The various arts that collaborate with the celebration of liturgy include architecture, painting, sculpture, music, choreography. Everything that participants see: lights and colors, the harmony of the space; everything they hear (presuming that the acoustics are suitable and functioning properly): voice, song, playing instruments; everything they smell: incense, perfumed oils like chrism; everything they taste: bread and wine; everything they touch: offering the sign of peace, kissing the gospel book, contact with the various objects in worship; and every movement they are engaged in: stational Masses, processions on Palm Sunday, Candlemas, and Rogation days[97]—everything about the liturgy presumes a creation focus.

A creation focus for liturgical theology will insist on the significance of symbolic engagement in worship as the chief means that liturgy has of experiencing (not just conceptualizing) God. This experience will naturally ground the ethical imperative of worship to revere and preserve creation. Further, a creation focus for the theology of liturgy and sacraments will ground the global relatedness of every act of worship, the paradigm for which is the annual Spring feast of Easter when the location of the moon and the rebirth of the earth provide the requisite cosmic context for the sacred rites of being reincorporated annually in the deepest sense possible in Christ's paschal mystery. Understandably this paradigm is much discussed in the context of liturgical inculturation since it presumes the locus of such a festival in the northern hemisphere. Although our concern here is to illustrate a classical association and coincidence, creation focus for liturgical theology is less grounded in the Spring/Easter combination than in emphasizing liturgy as an experience of God's "power and might" in continuing the salvific deeds of creation and redemption.

A creation focus for liturgical theology will ground the appropriateness of symbolic integrity and the fullness of symbolic interaction in the celebration of liturgy because it is through creation and symbolic elements that God is discovered, revealed, and encountered.[98] A creation focus for liturgical theology also necessarily implies and argues for the value of quality construction and the use of quality materials in church construction. Just as some liturgical symbols are the result of human ingenuity and productivity, so the construction of church buildings and liturgical spaces articulates the creative spirit and human manufacture intrinsic to the liturgy.[99]

A creation focus for the theology of liturgy can be used as one way to describe what occurs theologically in the liturgy of the word. Each time the word is proclaimed in the liturgical assembly the chaos and confusion that can dominate even an assembly of believers is overcome in the act of creation that is the liturgy of the word. And a creation focus for the theology of worship gives specificity to the *lex vivendi* because responding in life to what one celebrates necessarily includes environmental concerns.

A creation focus to liturgical theology may broaden categories of salvation that focus too intensely on an (individual or collective) experience of forgiveness to wider notions that include cosmic regeneration and renewal. The liturgy could be interpreted properly as the closest we can come here and now to what will only be perfected in the kingdom—the renewal of all things in heaven and earth and their recapitulation in Christ.[100] More particularly the Easter triduum would be a perfect setting for understanding liturgy as the way the human race overcomes paradise lost and experiences paradise regained. It could also appropriately image salvation as freedom for life in God on earth until the church enjoys eternal salvation in a "new heavens and new earth."

The primal celebration of earth, air, fire, and water that accompanies scripture readings such as the Genesis creation account (with its accompanying prayer), the Pauline exhortation to dying and rising with Christ in Romans 6:3–11, and the resurrection gospels—that begin "as the first day of the week was dawning" (Matthew 28:1) and "on the first day of the week at dawn" (Luke 24:1)—are important indications of the cosmic centeredness of this celebration and the appropriateness of drawing more fully on cosmic images for salvation.

Two particular examples from the Catholic tradition, Benedictine and Franciscan, are helpful indicators of the way an integral view of revering creation and of showing reverence for others in faith is intrinsically connected to liturgy. In a particularly compelling section of Chapter 31:9–11 of his *Rule*, St. Benedict asserts that the monastery cellarer shall show reverence for persons and things.

He must show every care and concern for the sick, children, guests, and the poor, knowing for certain that he will be held accountable for all of them on the day of judgment (9). He will regard all utensils and goods of the monastery as sacred vessels of the altar (10), aware that nothing is to be neglected (11).

This short statement, which reflects the thorough incarnationalism of the *Rule*, articulates the heart of Benedictine life in terms of seeing and revering all aspects of creation and human life. It also expresses the harmony between work and prayer that is proper to Benedictine monasticism. The striking role that showing reverence for the brethren and for the tools of the monastery has in the *Rule* is particularly noteworthy since cenobite monasticism places such a priority on liturgical prayer. A central idea and value in monasticism is thus the harmonious integration of all aspects of life seen from a particularly christological and incarnational perspective. In Benedictine monasticism

> Human life is a whole, and everything in creation is good. There is no aspect of life in this world that cannot, if rightly understood and used, contribute to leading us to our final end. Temporal reality and human endeavor are reflections of the perfections of God. Material things are *sacramenta*, symbols that reveal the goodness and beauty of the Creator. Consequently, Benedict can say that ordinary tools for work should be treated like the sacred vessels intended for liturgical use (31:10). It is only sin that has disfigured the beauty of creation and diverted things from their purpose. The monastic life is an effort to restore the lost paradise, to regain the image of God in man that has been distorted. Therefore the temporal order cannot be despised or neglected. In the monk's life there is no area that can be exempted from subjection to the divine precepts and the regime of grace. This is no disincarnate spirituality; conversion embraces the whole of life.[101]

The mendicant tradition of St. Francis of Assisi stands alongside the monastic as a helpful example of an integral view of the Christian life predicated on a wide notion of sacramentality and incarnationalism.[102] Pope John Paul II asserts as much:

> In 1979, I proclaimed Saint Francis of Assisi as the heavenly Patron of those who promote ecology.[103] He offers an example of genuine and deep respect for the integrity of creation. As a friend of the poor who was loved by God's creatures, Saint Francis invited all of creation—animal, plants, natural forces, even Brother Sun and Sister Moon—to give honor and praise to the Lord. The poor man of

Assisi gives us striking witness that when we are at peace with God we are better able to devote ourselves to building up that peace with all creation which is inseparable from peace among all peoples. It is my hope that the inspiration of St. Francis will help us to keep ever alive a sense of "fraternity" with all those good and beautiful things which almighty God has created. And may he remind us of our serious obligation to respect and watch over them with care, in light of that greater and higher fraternity that exists within the human family (n. 16).[104]

The Franciscan tradition's prizing of conventual liturgy (the eucharist and the hours), preaching, and their particular kind of communal life (among other things) stands as another significant example of how the principle of the sacramentality of human life functions in the Christian life as well as how the sacramentality of creation functions in this specific context.[105]

There are, at present, timely and significant convergences between creation theology and liturgical theology, which are particularly noted by (and also likely challenging) the Benedictine and Franciscan traditions.

CRITIQUE

In accord with the method I proposed in the beginning of this text, I now make some observations on the "critical function of liturgical theology" with regard to the way creation is described and used in the present reformed liturgy.

The first critique concerns texts. The eucharistic prayer, particularly its introductory section, is a classic locus for explicit reference to praise and thanks for creation.[106] Theologically, it leads to praising God for redemption, a section that is highly christological. In the present euchology, only the preface to the fourth eucharistic prayer contains any notable reference to praise for creation. While it can be granted that a highly christological emphasis has classically marked the Roman prefaces, it is certainly regrettable that the inroads in this direction signalled by the fourth eucharistic prayer were not more deeply made in the rest of the euchology.

Allied with this criticism is the debate often engaged in by liturgical theologians about what ought to be in a eucharistic prayer text and whether the anaphora should reflect general themes or a particular need. Some liturgists argued against the publication of eucharistic prayers for reconciliation and a preface for Masses in which the anointing of the sick takes place because such prayers focus too directly on a single theme. A possible loss to the structure and contents of the eucharistic prayer may be this praise motif when prefaces and eucharistic prayers for particular needs are developed.

A second critique concerns symbolic engagement in the revised rites and how the revised liturgy is celebrated. The issue concerns whether the contemporary Roman liturgy is sufficiently primal, explicitly related to creation and evocative of the produce and productivity of the earth. Roman Catholic eucharistic liturgy is all too frequently celebrated in a way that is more didactic than evocative, more educational than attitudinal, more informational than formational, more oriented toward learning than encounter, and more concerned with greater understanding than a progressively complete experience of assimilation into the mystery of God. A chief symptom here is the paradoxical situation in which the Roman Mass, previously noted for its "other-worldly" liturgy in terms of language, ritual, and gestural movement, and in particular the rites surrounding consecration, now finds itself with a comparatively overlong liturgy of the word. At the same time, the liturgy of the eucharist is flat and often seems to be a description of God, rather than a sensual and compelling evocation of God's mystery and otherness.

The issue is at least twofold: a disproportionate liturgy of the word and relatively minimal involvement of the assembly in symbolic (inter)action. Could it be that the theology of liturgy operative at present is too *christ*ological and *theo*logical in the sense that the primal and earthy aspects of liturgy are submerged in consciousness and not experienced sufficiently in the liturgical act? The celebration of the Easter vigil is the most striking example we have at present of a symbolically rich liturgy. However, if the overriding focus that night is on the incorporation of catechumens into the church by means of the Easter sacraments, certainly an important aspect of the revived rites of adult initiation, then what happens to the environmental context of this celebration in terms of the Spring renewal of the earth, the light of the moon and the reading of the Genesis creation account (among others) on which adult initiation is predicated? There is a clear danger here of ignoring the polyvalent meanings of this celebration and making them too catechumenal.

In point of fact, however, not all celebrations of the Easter vigil are concerned with the initiation of new adults. Such celebrations can contribute to acknowledging and broadening the theological appreciation of the vigil. For example, when the vigil is celebrated in a monastic community, it is obvious that the initiation of new members is less compelling than a theology of Easter that concerns renewing baptismal and monastic vows. In addition, if the monastic community happens to rely on farming for its livelihood, the celebration of the vigil may well be more adequately and obviously based on the renewal of the cosmos taking place in nature at that time. The very real yet symbolically imaged combat between God and Satan, redemption and condemnation, life and death, grace and sin, and virtue and temptation have a fuller meaning and take on a richer connotation when set within the cosmic struggle at this time of year when Spring strains to renew the earth and Winter hangs on to breathe its last. The cosmic battle between warmth and cold and between light and darkness provides the requisite and theologically rich context within which to consider the christologically and pneumatically rich theology of the Easter victory.

A final point to be made regarding symbolic engagement in the reformed liturgy concerns the absence as yet of any attention to the Rogation days that traditionally served as concrete demonstrations of the bond between altar and earth. The General Norms for the Liturgical Year and the Calendar state that Rogation and Ember days are days of particular intercession "for the needs of [all], especially for the productivity of the earth and [human] labor," (n. 45) and that the time and manner of these observations "should be determined by the episcopal conference" (n. 46). Especially at a time of rising ecological awareness and concern to fill the gap that all too often exists between liturgy and real life, it is regrettable that no action has yet been taken in these matters in the United States. Since the norms state that "the competent authority should set up norms for the extent of these celebrations" (n. 46), much latitude could be exercised to allow authentic and indigenous observances to mark these days when the church's prayer is explicitly concerned with creation and the things of the earth.

A third critique of the present Roman liturgy is the common overuse of hymns during the eucharist that are concerned with praising God. There is something repetitive, not to say redundant, in using hymns of praise, especially at the entrance and presentation of the gifts, because this motif is classically constitutive of the eucharistic prayer. "It is right to give him thanks and praise." A cause of this common error may be that we have yet to develop suitable musical theory and practice for the revised liturgy. In addition, the absence of hymns in the present *Missale Romanum* and *Antiphonale* for Mass (except for the Glory to God and Holy, holy, holy) indicates the problematic nature of any use of hymns at the eucharist. That praise themes dominate the hymns makes this phenomenon all the more regrettable.

A fourth critique concerns the sphere of aesthetics, a topic that deserves particular care in the selection of terms and categories. To agree that liturgy ought to be aesthetically pleasing and that its component elements should be qualitatively beautiful would not be difficult. A challenge to this statement could rightly be mounted if aesthetics is equated with ostentation and beauty merely with expense. Nuance and precision of argument is clearly necessary. It is also difficult to determine how aesthetics and beauty should be made intrinsic parts of the liturgical experience. But the lack of these qualities in the conduct of worship (despite the money spent) and in the construction of houses for worship requires that these matters be raised.

Too often the contemporary liturgy is criticized for a lack of beauty that can raise the human heart to God and a lack of artistic depth and integrity in church buildings, art, music, artifacts, vesture, and decorum in enactment. That these qualities may be prized for their own sake and be used derogatorily in worship are obvious dangers. However, it would be equally dangerous to relegate category of aesthetics or the category of beauty to relative nonimportance in planning and constructing churches or in the planning and celebration of liturgy. Theologically, liturgy presumes the contribution of the "work of human hands." Aesthetics requires that these works reflect high artistic standards in continuity with the premises on which the theology of liturgy is based and reflects the breadth of the Catholic tradition in terms of the use of art and architecture for worship.

A fifth critique draws on the observations made above that the present euchology and calendar reflect the northern hemisphere and ignore the experience of liturgical praying and feasting in the southern hemisphere. The argument in favor of composing a new euchology for the major seasons of Advent-Christmas-Epiphany and Lent-Easter-Pentecost rests on viewing the many traditional and time-honored euchological texts used at this time of year as paradigmatic of the theology of these feasts and seasons, not as literal norms. In fact, because this euchology would not be predicated on the passing of the longest nights of the year (Christmas) or the renewal of the earth in Spring (Easter), it could break ground in articulating the kind of hope believers have in viewing redemption as still to be completed. Eschatological yearning and hope from such euchology could serve the renewal of the church's euchology in both hemispheres.

A final critique concerns the contribution that concern for creation and the environment can make to the theology of the presentation of the gifts at the eucharist. Several recent studies in English have summarized the debate about the theological adequacy of these rites in the present reform and avenues for their further refinement in the Roman rite.[107] Most authors agree that the simplification of these rites from the Tridentine Missal was long overdue and that the present reform at least eliminates any kind of proleptic eucharistic prayer that had, unfortunately, burdened the former rite. The reform calls these rites the "preparation of the gifts" or the "preparation of the altar and the gifts"—not the "offertory." The simplified rites are a distinct improvement. The parallel texts "blessed are you, Lord God of all creation" are unfortunately problematic; like praise hymns at the eucharist, they reiterate what is explicitly and traditionally a central theological theme of the eucharistic prayer: to praise, bless, and thank God for the *mirabilia Dei*, especially as these continue to be experienced here and now through the eucharist.

An examination of the present rites of the preparation of the gifts reveal a too exclusive focus on the particular gifts of bread and wine, whereas reference to God's providence in providing all the goods of earth for nourishment and sustenance would be helpful. In addition, and more theologically pertinent, explicit reference to the contribution of human ingenuity, industry, and productivity in the manufacture of the elements of bread and wine is also missing. Not that I am arguing for a Pelagian-like theology of earning the gifts of salvation by work, but for some clear statement that the gifts presented represent a wealth of human productivity, including planting, harvesting, refining, making flour, pressing grapes, baking loaves of bread, and aging the fruit of the vine to become wine. Put somewhat differently, the theology reflected in this rite should take some cognizance of the fact that these polyvalent symbols, bread and wine, reflect the contribution of human productivity to the liturgy, as opposed to the use of symbols taken from nature such as water. In this connection, it is significant that the recently revised *Lutheran Book of Worship*[108] offers the following as one "offertory" hymn to be sung while "the Offering is received as the Lord's table is prepared" (n. 24).

> *Let the vineyards be fruitful, Lord,*
> *and fill to the brim our cup of blessing.*
> *Gather a harvest from the seeds that were sown,*
> *that we may be fed with the bread of life.*
> *Gather the hopes and dreams of all;*
> *unite them with the prayers we offer now.*
> *Grace our table with your presence,*
> *and give us a foretaste of the feast to come.*

In these days of ecumenical convergence and mutual enrichment, it is significant that this text says more theologically than do our double "blessed are you" prayers, and it is far more expansive in terms of evoking images of harvest and human productivity. It also offers an explicitly eschatological reference without which the focus of the rite can be limited to the presentation of this particular bread and wine. While the adoption of this text in the Roman rite would have its own set of problems, this example of Lutheran *lex orandi* affords a significant example of how ecumenical cooperation can offer insight and guidance for continuing liturgical revision and for developing the theological implications of revision.

This last contemporary critique of liturgical reform is an appropriate note on which to end and with which to indicate that what is argued here is for the wider Christian world. It is hoped that the particular contribution of the Roman Catholic tradition to these matters will help a wider Christian community validate the doctrine of the sacramentality of creation in worship. At the same time, it is hoped that the ecumenical convergence in liturgical and sacramental rites now emerging will lead to deepening convergence among the churches enabling the gap in the *lex credendi* between and among Christian churches to decrease.

NOTES

1. Not everyone who uses the original phrase understands it in the same way. An example is the debate on the weight that ought to be given to *statuat* in this formula: whether the church's prayer grounds belief, or belief grounds the formulas for liturgical prayer, or a mutual influence is operative between prayer and belief. This debate is reflected in Geoffrey Wainwright's review of Kavanagh's *On Liturgical Theology* in *Worship* 61(2): 183, 183–6. (Some contemporary authors prefer to use the shortened phrase *lex orandi, lex credendi*.)

2. The authorship of this phrase, found in the so-called *Capitula coelestini* (statements added to a letter of Pope Celestine I dated in the early fifth century [P.L. 51:205–212] also called the *Capitula* or *Auctoritates de gratia*) is now generally ascribed to Prosper of Aquitaine. See M. Cappuyns, L'origine des Capitula pseudo-célestiniens contre le semi-pélagianisme. *Revue Bénédictine.* 41(2): 156–70; Paul De Clerck, "Lex *orandi, lex credendi*: Sens originel et avatars historiques d'un adage équivoque." *Questions Liturgiques* 59(3): 193–212, and "*La prière universelle dans les liturgiques latines anciennes. Témoinages patristiques et textes liturgiques.* Liturgiewissenschaftliche Quellen und Forschungen. 62 (Münster: Aschendorff, 1977), 88–89. See also what is generally regarded as a "classic" commentary and analysis, Karl Federer, *Liturgie und Glaube, Eine theologiegeschichtliche Untersuchung.* Paradosis IV. Legem credendi lex statuat supplicandi (Fribourg: Paulusverlag, 1950), 19–41. On the original text and a standard interpretation of its usefulness for liturgical theology see Mario Righetti. *Manuale di storia liturgica.* 4 volumes. 2d. edition (Milano: Ancora, 1950), 1:25–27.

3. See Mark Searle, "Renewing the liturgy—Again," *Commonweal* 140(2): 617–22. In this same connection see the introduction and collected essays in *Liturgie—Ein vergessenes Thema der Theologie?* ed. Klemens Richter (Freiburg: Basel, 1987). Undoubtedly the statement of the Liturgy Constitution has influenced some of this work:

> The study of liturgy is to be ranked among the compulsory and major courses in seminaries and religious houses of studies; in theological faculties it is to rank among the principal subjects. It is to be taught under its theological, historical, pastoral, and juridical aspects (n. 16).

For an overview of the historical evolution of this aspect of liturgical study, see Kevin W. Irwin, *Liturgical Theology: A Primer.* (Collegeville, MN: The Liturgical Press, 1990), 11–17; "Sacrament," in *New Dictionary of Theology,* ed. Joseph A. Komonchak et al. (Wilmington, DE: Glazier, 1987), 910–22; and *Context and Text* (Collegeville, MN: Liturgical Press, 1993).

4. See among others the writings of Alexander Schmemann, Cipriano Vagaggini, Irénée H. Dalmais, and Salvatore Marsili. For an overview see my *Liturgical Theology,* 19–29, 40–44 and the bibliography, 74–77.

5. Among these, the work of Albert Houssiau and Gerard Lukken is particularly important. See *Liturgical Theology,* 29–34, and the bibliography, 75–76.

6. See among others, Pedro Fernandez, "Liturgia y teología. Una cuestion metodologica," *Ecclesia Orans* 6(3): 261–83.

7. A comparison of the former Roman Ritual for baptism with the post-Vatican II revised rites yields important insight on this matter. For example, the introduction to the former rite describes valid administration "by pouring the water, or by immersion or by sprinkling" (Philip T. Weller, ed., *The Roman Ritual.* [Milwaukee: Bruce Publishing Co., 1964], 34, n.10). The rite itself presents the formula and the rubrics together: "N., I baptize you in the name of the Father (here he pours the first time) and of the Son, (pouring a second time) and of the Holy Spirit (pouring a third time" [nn. 19, 58]). The present General Instruction on Christian Initiation states that "as the rite for baptizing, either immersion, which is more suitable as a symbol of participation in the death and resurrection of Christ, or pouring may lawfully be used" (n. 11). The rite itself separates the two forms, placing immersion first (n. 226).

8. The terms "adaptation," "accommodation," and "inculturation" are variously defined and understood. The descriptions offered by Anscar J. Chupungco have been influential. See *Cultural Adaptation of the Liturgy* (New York: Paulist, 1988); *Liturgies of the Future* (New York: Paulist, 1990); Toward a Definition of Inculturation," *Ecclesia Orans* 5(1): 11–29; and "Popular Religiosity and Liturgical Inculturation," *Ecclesia Orans* 8(1): 97–115. Another author whose work has been very influential in this area is D.S. Amalorpavadass. See "Theological Thoughts on Inculturation," *Studia Liturgica* 20(1): 36–54, 116–36.

9. A particularly useful statement of the need for a new method in liturgical theology based on ritual studies as a relatively new discipline and one that is germane to our argument is Theodore W. Jennings, "Ritual Studies and Liturgical Theology: An Invitation to Dialogue," *Journal of Ritual Studies* 1(1):

35–56. Important examples of this methodological approach include the past and ongoing work of two study groups in the North American Academy of Liturgy, the "Liturgy and Social Sciences" and "Liturgy and Ritual Studies." On the European side, an important example is the method developed and exemplified in the Pastoral Liturgy Institute of Santa Giustina in Padua, Italy. See the important publications from this Institute, especially R. Cecolin, A.N. Terrin and P. Visentin, editors, *Una liturgia per l'uomo. La liturgia pastorale e i suoi compiti* «Caro Salutis Cardo». Studi 5. Padova: Edizioni Messagero. 1986; the monograph on method by Giorgio Bonaccorso, *Introduzione Allo Studio Della Liturgia.* «Caro Salutis Cardo». Sussidi 1. Padova: Edizioni Messagero. 1990; and the two volume summary of the work of Pelagio Visentin, ed. R. Cecolin and F. Trolese, *Culmen et fons, Raccolta di Studi di Liturgia e Spiritualità.* «Caro Salutis Cardo». Studi 3 and 4. Padova: Edizioni Messagero. 1987.

10. See Mary Collins, "Critical Questions for Liturgical Theology," *Worship* 53(4): 302–17; "Liturgical Methodology and the Cultural Evolution of Worship in the United States," *Worship* 49(2): 85–102; "The Public Language of Ministry, *Official Ministry in a New Age*, in Permanent Seminar Studies. No. 3 ed. James H. Provost (Washington: Canon Law Society of America, 1981), 7–40.

11. On this comparatively new and underexplored aspect of liturgical method, see among others, Angelus Haussling, "Die kritische Funktion der Liturgiewissenschaft," in Hans B. Meyer, ed. *Liturgie und Gesellschaft* (Innsbruck: Tyrolia Verlag, 1970), 103–30; David N. Power, "Cult to Culture: The Liturgical Foundation of Theology," *Worship* 54(6): 482–95; and "People at Liturgy." *Twenty Years of Concilium—Retrospect and Prospect*, Concilium 170 (Edinburgh: T. and T. Clark, 1983), 8–14; and Mary Collins, "The Public Language of Ministry."

12. For an overview of the important contributions made in this area in the present century, see Franco Brovelli, "Movimento liturgico e spiritualita liturgica," *Rivista Liturgica* 73(4): 469–90. Particularly notable are the works of Cipriano Vagaggini, Lambert Beauduin, and Romano Guardini.

13. See, one example Matias Auge, Le messe «pro sancta ecclesia»: Un' espressione della «lex orandi» in sintonia con la «lex credendi» e la «lex vivendi.» *Notitiae* 26(8): 566–84.

14. This life-relation of liturgy has been given added stimulus in contemporary discourse by liberation theologians who theologize about the ethical demands of the Christian faith in situations that hinder or actually inhibit the development of the Christian life as taught by Jesus and experienced in liturgy. The challenge to live as we celebrate may mean critiquing and revitalizing oppressive social structures. It may also mean emphasizing individual commitments to reform oneself as well as structures of society.

15. See Bernard J. Leeming, *Principles of Sacramental Theology* (London/ New York: Longmans Green, 1956), 601 fn.41. Leeming states that "The *Catechism of the Council of Trent* gives seven reasons to show the fitness of sacraments to man's present condition [the first of which is]: (1) visible signs fit man's dual nature of body and soul."

16. David N. Power. *Unsearchable Riches: The Symbolic Nature of the Liturgy* (New York: Pueblo Publishing Co, 1984). See Bernard J. Leeming, *Principles of Sacramental Theology*, 600.

. . . in simple things God is to be found: in the authority of human beings, in words spoken by men, in water, bread, oil, wine, and human gesture. Man is reminded that he is not pure spirit, and that his holiness must consist, as it is found, in the sanctity of both body and soul, in both the spiritual and the material.

17. See Louis-Marie Chauvet, *Symbole et sacrement: Une relecture sacramentelle de l'existence chrétienne* (Paris: Cerf, 1987), 195–232.

18. See Gordon Lathrop, *"Holy Things: Foundations for Liturgical Theology." Institute of Liturgical Studies.* No. 7 (Valparaiso: Valparaiso Institute, 1991). He makes this helpful comment about the eucharist: "The meal is both the thanksgiving and the eating and drinking. The thanksgiving prayer gives words to what happens in communion. The eating and drinking is always more than the prayer can say" (p. 35).

19. For example, regarding the use of water in baptism, the section of the blessing prayer referring to the Genesis account of Noah's ark regards it most positively and as a victory ("the waters of the great flood you made a sign of the waters of baptism that make an end to sin and a new beginning of goodness") whereas the event itself can be interpreted on many other levels, some of which reflect a negative judgment against sinful humanity.

20. In what follows, the "bread and wine" terminology is used for convenience, not to settle the argument about appropriate elements for the eucharist.

21. *De carnis resurrectione.* Corpus scriptorum ecclesiasticorum latinorum 47(9), 25–125. See Cipriano Vagaggini, *Caro salutis est cardo—Corporetá, eucaristia e liturgia* (Rome: Desclee, 1966). It is also noteworthy that this phrase of Tertullian is the title of the series from the Santa Giustina Liturgical Institute of Padua (see note 9).

22. See Karl Rahner, "The Presence of Christ in the Sacrament of the Lord's Supper," *Theological Investigations* 4, trans. Kevin Smyth (Baltimore: Helicon Press, 1966), 309.

23. For a helpful summary of the importance of the epiclesis in contemporary Roman Catholic and other churches' eucharistic prayers, see John H. McKenna, "The epiclesis revisited," *New Eucharistic Prayers: An Ecumenical Study of Their Development and Structure,* ed. Frank C. Senn (New York: Paulist Press, 1987), 169–94.

24. Translation from R.C.D. Jasper and G.J. Cuming, *Prayers of the Eucharist: Early and Reformed.* 3d revised ed. (New York: Pueblo Publishing Co, 1987), 24.

25. A generally helpful summary of Karl Rahner's thought in this regard occurs in Michael Skelley, *The Liturgy of the World* (Collegeville: The Liturgical Press / A Pueblo Book, 1991), 85–158.

26. See the Ecumenical forum, "Creation and Culture: An Ecumenical Challenge," *The Ecumenical Review* 37(4): 506–11, quoting the Orthodox theologian Emilie Dierking Lisenko who

> pointed to the spiritual/material dualism, and to a certain arrogance against nature. In the Eastern Christian vision God did not create the world for the sake of human welfare per se and

thus for exploitation, but as an element for human communication with God, the human person being a priest for eucharistic
celebration of the world. Liturgy comprehends the whole of creation and shows definitely a communal orientation! The Fall
expresses human love for the world as an end in itself, separating it from God and thus from its very source of life. Nature is
not evil, salvation is for all of creation (507).

And citing Harold Ditmanson:

Everything exists because God existed first. Therefore grace is
prior to creation. The world has only a relative independence,
and is—in its goodness—God's self-expression. Nothing in creation is essentially unclean. Sin is a secondary concept, and
redemption means restoration. Some idea of a continuous creation is necessary. Nature must be seen as a single coherent
event (510).

27.   Michael J. Himes and Kenneth R. Himes, "The sacrament of Creation," *Commonweal* 142(2): 44–45.

28.   See Jürgen Moltmann's interesting thesis, "The Sabbath: The Feast
of Creation," in *God in Creation. A New Theology of Creation and the Spirit of God*
(San Francisco: Harper and Row, 1985), 276–95, and the Appendix: "Symbols
of the world," 297–28.

29.   The presumption in this section is the experience of light/ darkness
and the seasons in the northern hemisphere. In the final ("critique") section of
this paper much more will be said about possibilities for varied euchology
based on other ways daylight and the seasons are experienced.

30.   There are five Mass formulas for "VII Kalens Iulias Natale Sancti
Iohannis Baptistae" in the Verona Collection. See *Sacramentarium Veronense,
Rerum ecclesiasticarum documenta 1.* L. Cunibert Mohlberg et. al., eds. (Rome:
Herder. 1978), Nn. 232–56.

31.   Insightful descriptions of the *lucernarium* and its influence on Chris-
tian vespers are found in Paul Bradshaw. *Daily Prayer in the Early Church*
(New York: Oxford University Press, 1982), 22, 51, 57, 75–77, 80, 116, 119, 135.
George Guiver, *Company of Voices: Daily Prayer and the People of God* (New
York: Pueblo, 1988), 62–66, 202–3; and Robert Taft, *The Liturgy of the Hours in
East and West* (Collegeville: The Liturgical Press, 1986), 26–28, 36–38, 55–56,
211–12, 355–56.

32.   One of the disadvantages in the proposal to establish a "fixed date"
for Easter (largely for ecumenical purposes) is the fact that this would miti-
gate the sense of relying on cosmic rhythms to establish its dating.

33.   See Bernhard W. Anderson, "Creation in the Bible," in Philip N.
Joranson, ed. *Cry of the Environment* (Santa Fe: Bear and Co., 1984):

The doctrine of creation, then, underlines and validates the
truth that history, from beginning to end, is under the sovereign
purpose of God as revealed in Jesus Christ. The Fourth Gospel
begins by echoing the opening words of Genesis: "In the beginning" and speaks about the light shining in darkness (cf. 2
Corinthians 4:6). And even as Christ was in the beginning, so

he will triumph at the end (1 Corinthians 15:24–28; Revelation [40]).

34. All the English translations of texts presented here are from the International Committee on English in the Liturgy (hereafter ICEL) texts now in use. That these translations will be adjusted in the new edition of the Sacramentary is almost certain. The Latin original of this prayer is from the former Roman missal. See Pierre Bruylants, *Les oraisons du missel Romain* (Louvain: Abbeye de Mont César, 1952), N. 347.

35. From former Roman usage, P. Bruylants, *Les Oraisons,* n. 176.

36. From former Roman usage, originally from the Hadrianum. See Jean Deshusses, *Le sacramentaire Grégorien* (Fribourg: Editions Universitaires, 1979), N. 51.

37. From the Leonine sacramentary, *Sacramentarium Vernonense.* N. 1260.

38. From former Roman usage, from a combination of two sacramentary texts: *Sacramentarium Veronense,* N. 1247, and the old Gelasian sacramentary, *Liber sacramentorum Romanae ecclesiae ordinis anni circuli.* ed. L. C. Mohlberg, Rerum Ecclesiasticarum Documenta IV (Rome: Herder, 1960), N. 59.

39. See among others Gerhard von Rad. *Old Testament Theology* 1, trans. D.M.G. Stalker (New York: Harper and Row, 1962), 15–35; and John Bright, *A History of Israel* (Philadelphia: Westminster, 1959). Bright states that

> Unleavened Bread (and Passover), Weeks, and Ingathering . . . were far older than Israel and, save for Passover, were agricultural in origin. Israel borrowed them [and] gave them a new rationale by imparting to them a historical content. They ceased to be mere nature festivals and became occasions when the mighty acts of Yahweh toward Israel were celebrated. Presumably these feasts were for practical reasons celebrated at local shrines as well as at Shiloh. But there is evidence of a great annual feast at Shiloh to which godly Israelites repaired (Judges 21:19; 1 Samuel 1:3, 21). Though we are not told, this was probably the autumn feast of Ingathering and the turn of the year. It is exceedingly probable, too, and very likely in connection with this annual feast, that there was a regular ceremony of covenant renewal (Deuteronomy 31:9–13) . . . (148).

40. It is not coincidental that the continuous reading from Revelation occurs in the Office of Readings in the Liturgy of the Hours from Monday of the Second Week of Easter through Saturday of the Fifth Week of Easter and as the second reading at Mass during the Easter season "C" cycle indicating that Easter is a season of rebirth and sharing of the first fruits of the resurrection.

41. That creation can serve the mediating function of coming to know God is also explicitly confirmed through the New Testament. A classic text used to support the notion that creation can lead to knowledge of God is Romans 1:19–20:

> "in fact whatever can be known about God is clear to them; he himself made it so. Since the creation of the world, invisible

realities, God's eternal power and divinity, have become visible, recognizable through the things he has made. Romans 1:25 ("the Creator . . . is blessed forever") is printed in the present text of the liturgy of the hours as the phrase that can be meditated on when praying the canticle of Daniel 3:52–57 at Sunday morning prayer.

42. Besides these hymns for ferial evening prayer, a number of other texts, prescribed for use in the former Breviary, are similarly inspired by or refer to creation. Among them: *Creator alme siderum*, vespers Sundays and weekdays of Advent; *Audi benigne conditor*, vespers Sundays and weekdays of Lent; *Quem terra, pontus, sidera*, matins of the Blessed Virgin Mary without a proper matins hymn; *Rerum creator optime*, Wednesday matins; *Rerum Deus tenax vigor*, none throughout the year; *Salutis humanae sator*, vespers Ascension to Pentecost; *Aeterne rerum conditor*, Sunday lauds; *Ecce jam noctis*, Sunday lauds; *Splendor paternae gloriae*, Monday lauds; *Primo die, quo Trinitas*, Sunday matins; *O sol salutis, intimis*, Lent lauds; *Rex sempiterne coelitum*, matins Eastertide; *Veni creator Spiritus*, vespers and terce on Pentecost and through octave. See *The Hymnal for the Hours* (Chicago: Gregorian Institute of America, 1989), Nn. 148–157; and *The Summit Choirbook* (Summit: Dominican Nuns, 1983), Nn. 179–186, for vesper hymns translated into English and set to various metrical settings.

43. All English translations are from Matthew Britt, *The Hymns of the Breviary and Missal* (New York: Benziger Brothers, 1922), 74.

44. Each of these hymns is discussed in succession in Britt, *The Hymns*, 73–85, with Latin and English texts, notes on authorship and a theological commentary.

45. Martien E. Binkman, "A Creation Theology for Canberra?" *The Ecumenical Review* 42(2): 150–56. Binkman asserts that creation is no longer preeminently bound to the first person of the Trinity but to the third person, and that here the bond between Christ and the Spirit is emphasized. Therefore we cannot, for example, casually substitute the Son (Christology) in creation theology with the Spirit (Pneumatology).

46. The text (from Britt, *The Hymns*) is:
> As fades the glowing orb of day,
> To Thee, great source of light, we pray;
> Blest Three in One, to every heart
> Thy beams of life and love impart.
> At early dawn, at close of day,
> To Thee our vows we humbly pay;
> May we, mid joys that never end,
> With Thy bright Saints in homage bend (84).

47. *Sun and moon, bless the Lord;*
> *stars of heaven, bless the Lord.*
> *Every shower and dew, bless the Lord;*
> *all you winds, bless the Lord (62–64).*

48. *Blessed are you, and praiseworthy,*
> *O Lord, the God of our Fathers,*
> *and glorious forever is your name.*

> *For you are just in all you have done;*
> > *all your deeds are faultless,*
> > *all your ways right (26–27).*

49. *Hannaniah, Azariah, Mishael,*
> > *bless the Lord praise and exalt him above all forever.*
> *For he has delivered us from the nether world,*
> > *and saved us from the power of death;*
> *he has freed us from the raging flame*
> > *and delivered us from the fire.*
> *Give thanks to the Lord, for he is good,*
> > *for his mercy endures forever.*
> *Bless the God of gods,*
> > *all you who fear the Lord;*
> *praise him and give him thanks,*
> > *because his mercy endures forever (88–90).*

50. The General Instruction on the Liturgy of the Hours states: "The psalmody of morning prayer consists of one morning psalm, then a canticle from the Old Testament, and finally a second psalm of praise, following the tradition of the Church (n. 43)."

51. *Come, let us sing to the Lord*
> > *and shout with joy to the Rock who saves us.*
> *Let us approach him with praise and thanksgiving*
> > *and sing joyful songs to the Lord.*
> *The Lord is God, the mighty God,*
> > *the great king over all the gods.*
> *He holds in his hands the depths of the earth*
> > *and the highest mountains as well.*
> *He made the sea; it belongs to him,*
> > *the dry land too, for it was formed by his hands*
> *Come, then, let us bow down and worship,*
> > *bending the knee before the Lord, our maker*
> *For he is our God and we are his people,*

See B. Anderson, "Creation":

> Creation is the foundation of the covenant; it provides the setting within which Yahweh's saving work takes place. But it is equally true that creation is embraced within the theological meaning of covenant. Therefore psalmists may regard creation as the first of God's saving deeds (Psalm 74:12–17) and in the recitation of the *Heilgeschichte* may move without a break from the deeds of creation to historical deeds of liberation (Psalm 136 [26]).

52. See B. Anderson, "Creation":

> It seems, then, that Israel's earliest traditions did not refer to Yahweh as creator in a cosmic sense but concentrated, rather, on Yahweh's "mighty deeds" of liberation, through which the Holy God became known and formed Israel as a people out of the chaos of historical oblivion and oppression (23f).

53. A significant example of how contemporary liturgical scholarship has rediscovered and appropriated the Jewish cultic terms *berakah* and *todah*

as central to understanding the eucharistic prayer are in Cesare Giraudo, *La struttura letteraria della preghiera eucaristica. Saggio sullagenesi letteraria di una forma. Toda* veterotestamentaria *Berakah* giudaica. Anafora cristiana (Rome: Biblical Institute Press, 1981); and *Eucaristia per la Chiesa.* Prospettive teologiche sulla l'eucaristia a partire della «lex orandio» (Rome: Gregorian University Press, 1989). A much earlier use of the *berakah* to explain the theology of the eucharistic prayer is in Louis Bouyer, *Eucharist* (Notre Dame, IN: University of Notre Dame Press, 1968), 15–135. Bouyer relies on earlier scholars such as J. P. Audet.

54. Gail Ramshaw-Schmidt, *Christ in Sacred Speech* (Philadelphia: Fortress Press, 1986), 77–78.

55. The use of "classic" indicates those elements that are most generally found in eucharistic prayers in the tradition. It is not meant to suggest that there is but one model for eucharistic praying. In fact a review of these prayers discloses much variation within the commonly agreed upon anaphoral structure. See, for example, the useful overview of these ritual and theological differences in Hans Bernhard Meyer, *Eucharistie, Geschichte, Theologie, Pastoral: Handbuch der Liturgiewissenschaft* 4 (Regensburg: Friedrich Pustet, 1989), esp. Chapter 3, Vom Herrenmahl zur Eucharistiefeier, and Chapter 4, Die Ritusfamilien des Ostens und des Westens, 87–164. A helpful comparison summary of the Antiochean and Alexandrian anaphoral structure is on page 133. For a collection of such texts and appropriate comparisons within and among liturgical families, see Anton Hanggi and Irmgard Pahl, *Prex eucharistica: Textus e variis liturgiis antiquioribus selecti* (Fribourg: Editions Universitaires, 1968), and the translations in R. C .D. Jasper and G. J. Cuming, *Prayers of the Eucharist.*

56. That this motif is underexplored in the present reformed liturgy will be explained in section five.

57. Louis Bouyer argues that the sources for this prayer are Eastern and include the *Apostolic Constitutions*, the Liturgy of St. James and of St. Basil. See *Eucharist*, 448.

58. Joseph Keenan, "The Importance of the Creation Motif in the Eucharistic Prayer" *Worship* 53(4): 341–56.

59. B. Anderson, "Creation":
> Although all God's creatures are summoned to praise their Creator, human beings are the only earthlings in whom praise can become articulate. They are made for conversation with God, for a dialogue in an I-and-thou relation. . . . Israel's calling is to vocalize the praise that wells up from all peoples and nations (34).

60. J. Keenan, "The Importance of the Creation Motif," 349.

61. The full text is found in A. Hanggi and I. Pahl, *Prex eucharistica.* 82–95; see also Jasper-Cuming, *Prayers of the Eucharist,* 104–13.

62. See B. Anderson, "Creation":
> Apparently Canaanite mythology does not deal with creation in the cosmic sense but with the maintenance of the created order in the face of the periodic threats of chaos. . . . The OT con-

tains reminiscences of these ancient myths of creation against chaos (44).

He then cites Herman Gunkel, "The Influence of Babylonian Mythology upon the Biblical Creation Story," Charles A. Muenchow, trans., in B. W. Anderson, ed. *Creation in the Old Testament* (Philadelphia: Fortress Press, 1984), 25–52; and Anderson, *Creation Versus Chaos: The Reinterpretation of Mythical Symbolism in the Bible* (New York: Association Press, 1967), Chapter One.

63. On this term in the history of religions and why it was repeated annually, most usually in the Spring, see Mircea Eliade, *Cosmos and Myth* trans. Willard Trask (New York: Harper Torchbooks, 1959).

64. On the intrinsic connection among these things, see Susan Power Bratton, "Christian Ecotheology and the Old Testament," *Environmental Ethics* 6(2): 195–209.

65. B. Anderson, "Creation", 29–30: "Creation by the Word came to be the normative expression of the mode of God's creative work . . . . God's Word is an act, an event, a sovereign command, which accomplishes a result. The creation story affirms that God's Word, mighty in history, is also the very power which brought the creation into being. Since the creative Word establishes a personal relationship between the creator and the creation, the Christian faith affirms with theological consistency that the Logos (Word) became flesh in a person (John 1:1–18).

66. Here is the Latin original (of the first prayer after the creation account):

> *Omnipotens sempiterne Deus,*
> *qui es in omnium operum tuorum dispensations mirabilis,*
> *intelligant redempti tui, non fuisse excellentius,*
> *quod initio factus est mundus,*
> *quam quod in fine saeculorum*
> *Pascha nostrum immolatus est Christus.*

The source for this prayer is the previous Roman Missal. See P. Bruylants, *Les oraisons*, n. 385.

67. A review of the Latin text of this second (i.e., alternative) prayer yields something of the balance customarily found in Latin collects, which text is from the former Roman Missal. See P. Bruylants, *Les oraisons*:

> *Deus, qui mirabiliter creasti hominem*
> *et mirabilius redemisti,*
> *da nobis, quaesumus,*
> *contrea oblectamenta peccati mentis ratione presistere,*
> *ut mereamur ad aeterna gaudia prevenire.*
> *Per Christum Dominum nostrum (n. 786).*

68. A comparison of the titles for God in the present Latin *Missale Romanum* reveals that among the most frequently used terms, *omnipotens*, is used 277 times, whereas *creator* is used 5 times. See Thaddaus A. Schnitker and Wolfgang A. Slaby, *Concordantia Verbalia Missalis Romani* (Westfalen: Aschendorff Munster, 1983), Col. 398–399, 1704–16.

69. In *Christ in Sacred Speech*, page 30, Gail Ramshaw-Schmidt states:

> Thus at the beginning of the Great Thanksgiving, we pray

along with Abraham who obeyed the call (Genesis 12:4), with Moses, who received the Torah (Exodus 19:20), and with Jesus, who was the Word (John 1:1). As we eat bread and wine, we recall Abraham, who shared his food with three mysterious visitors (Genesis 18:8), Moses, who ate and drank with God on Sinai and did not die (Exodus 24:11), and Jesus, who breaking bread on Sunday evening, showed forth his wounds (Luke 24:31).

70. See among others Jürgen Moltmann, *The Future of Creation: Collected Essays*, trans. Margaret Kohl (Philadelphia: Fortress Press, 1979), 119–30.

71. See Edward J. Kilmartin, *Christian Liturgy* (Kansas City: Sheed and Ward, 1988), especially 100–199; and Jean Corbon, *The Wellspring of Worship*, trans. Matthew O'Connell (New York: Paulist Press, 1988).

72. Because of weaknesses in the present ICEL translation, the Latin text is particularly illustrative:

> *Vere sanctus es, Domine,*
> *et merito te laudat omnis a te condita creatura,*
> *quia per Filium tuum,*
> *Dominum nostrum Iesum Christum,*
> *Spiritus Sancti operante virtute,*
> *vivificas et sanctificas universa,*
> *et populum tibi congregare non desinis,*
> *ut a solis ortu usque ad occasum*
> *oblatio munda offeratur nomini tuo.*

73. The Latin reads:

> *Haec ergo dona, quaesumus,*
> *Spiritus tui ruore sanctifica,*
> *ut nobis Corpus et Sanguinis fiant*
> *Domine nostri Iesu Christi.*

> *Et supplices deprecamur*
> *ut Corporis et Sanguinis Christi participes*
> *a Spiritu Sancto congregemur in unum.*

74. This assertion is not to ignore the difficulty some liturgists have with the present "split epiclesis," that is the now separate invocations for the transformation of the gifts and the intercession for the church.

75. See Cinette Ferriere, "A propos de *Dieu-potier* Images de la création et foi chrétienne en Dieu créateur," *Paroisse et Liturgie* 48(6): 533–48.

76. See J. Moltmann, *God in Creation*, 9–13; and Lukas Vischer, "Giver of Life—Sustain your Creation!" *The Ecumenical Review* 42(2): 143–49.

77. For example, Phillipians 2:6–11, Colossians 1:15–20, 1 Timothy 3:16. See B. Anderson, "Creation," 41–42: Jesus Christ is the "likeness of God" (2 Corinthians 4:4) and the "image of the invisible God, the first-born of all creation" (Colossians 1:15). This language recalls the "image of God" in Genesis 1:26 just as Hebrews 2:5–9 interprets the "man" who is "crowned with glory and honor" (Psalm 8:4–6) christologically.

78. See Jordi Gilbert Tarruell, Los formularios de la benedicion del agua en el «Ordo Baptismi Parvolorum» y en el «Ordo Initiationis Christianae Adultorum». *Ephemerides Liturgicae* 88(4): 275–309; and the recent study in English by Mark Searle, "*Fons vitae*: A Case Study in the use of Liturgy as a Theological Source," in *Fountain of Life*, ed. Gerard Austin (Washington: Pastoral Press, 1991), 217–42, an important essay in the methodology of liturgical theology; and Dominic E. Serra, "The Blessing of Baptismal Water at the Paschal Vigil in the Post-Vatican II Rite," *Ecclesia Orans* 7(3): 343–68.

79. The General Instructions and Rites of Christian Initiation for Adults and for Children are introduced by another document called the General Instruction [on] Christian Initiation (hereafter GICI). All quotations from General Instruction on Christian Initiation and from the adult rite of initiation (RCIA) are from the ICEL translation of 1988. The numbering cited is that used in the *Study Edition* (Chicago: Liturgy Training Publications, 1988).

80. The second form of the blessing prayer also capitalizes on the notion of washing by asking God to

> *Make holy this water which you have created,*
> *so that all who are baptized in it may be washed clean of sin*
> *and born again to live as your children (222 B).*

81. *Grant that these catechumens,*
> *who, like the woman of Samaria,*
> *thirst for living water (154 A).*
> *Now, by your power,*
> *free these elect from the cunning of Satan,*
> *as they draw near to the fountain of living water (154 B).*

82. *Deepen the faith and understanding*
> *of these elect, chosen for baptism.*
> *Give them new birth in your living waters,*
> *so that they may be numbered among your adopted children (182).*

83. Sebastian P. Brock has investigated these rites and forwarded interesting theses. See "The Consecration of Water in the Oldest Manuscripts of the Syrian Orthodox Baptismal Liturgy," *Orientalia Christiana Periodica* 37(2): 317–32.

84. *Your Son willed that water and blood should flow from his side as he hung upon the cross (222 A).*

> *Praise to you, Lord Jesus Christ, the Father's only Son,*
> *for you offered yourself on the cross,*
> *that in the blood and water flowing from your side*
> *and through your death and resurrection*
> *the Church might be born (222 B; repeated in 222 D).*

85. *The God of power and Father of Our Lord Jesus Christ*
> *has freed you from sin*
> *and brought you to new life*
> *through water and the Holy Spirit.*
> *He now anoints you with the chrism of salvation,*

> *so that, united with his people,*
> *you may remain for ever a member of Christ*
> *who is Priest, Prophet and King (228).*

This prayer refers to the important notions of remaining "a member of Christ who is Priest, Prophet and King" which remain left out of the celebration if confirmation follows immediately. In our judgment the inclusion of this statement into the sequence of water—baptism-confirmation-first eucharist at the Easter Vigil would be a helpful adjustment to this rite.

86. The reference here is specific in that our concern is with what occurs because of the use of water, not what occurs through the use of any other symbolic gestures or elements, such as tracing the cross, imposing hands, kiss of peace, or the use of the oil of catechumens, chrism, and bread and wine.

87. The footnote to this text cites Romans 8:15, Galatians 4:5, Trent Denziger. 1524. 796. Our concern here is not to describe in full all the results of baptism as, for example, those listed in GICI 5, but merely to indicate the results of using the symbol of water or in tests that refer to the use of water.

88. As seen in the texts, thus:

> *May he give them the new life of the Holy Spirit*
> *whom we are about to call down upon this water (220).*

> *Praise to you, almighty God and Father,*
> *for you have created water to cleanse and give life (222 D).*

> *By water and the Holy Spirit*
> *you freed your sons and daughters from sin*
> *and gave them new life (234).*

> *By the power of the Holy Spirit*
> *give to this water the grace of your Son,*
> *so that in the sacrament of baptism*
> *all those whom you have created in your likeness*
> *may be cleansed from sin*
> *and rise to a new birth of innocence . . . (222 A).*

> *You have called your children, N. and N.,*
> *to this cleansing water and new birth . . . (222 C,D,E).*
> *We pray for these your servants,*
> *who eagerly approach the waters of new birth*
> *and hunger for the banquet of life (175 B).*

> *Let us pray for these elect, that God in his mercy may make them responsive to his love, so that through the waters of rebirth they may receive pardon for their sins and have life in Christ Jesus our Lord (182).*

> *Give them new birth in your living waters,*
> *so that they may be numbered among your adopted children(182).*

As proclaimed in the prayers for the blessing of the water, baptism is a cleansing water of rebirth that makes us God's children born from on high (GICI, 5).

89. Philippe Rouillard, "From Human Meal to Christian Eucharist," in *Living Bread, Saving Cup: Readings on the Eucharist*, ed. R. Kevin Seasoltz (Collegeville: The Liturgical Press, 1982), 126. This article appeared originally in *Notitiae* (1977), Nn. 131–32.

90. See Philippe Rouillard, "From Human Meal to Christian Eucharist."

91. The general instruction on the Roman Missal states that "following the example of Christ, the Church has always used bread and wine with water to celebrate the Lord's Supper" (n. 281). It then states:

> The nature of the sign demands that the material for the eucharistic celebration truly have [sic] the appearance of food. [E]ven though unleavened and baked in the traditional shape, the eucharistic bread should be made in such a way that . . . the priest is able actually to break the host into parts and distribute them to at least some of the faithful. . . . The action of the breaking of the bread, the simple term for the eucharist in apostolic times, will more clearly bring out the force and meaning of the sign of the unity of all in the one bread and of their charity, since the one bread is being distributed among the members of one family (n. 283).

92. See Jerome Murphy O'Connor, "Eucharist and Community in 1 Corinthians," in *Living Bread*, 1–30. For important patristic sources, see Willy Rordorf, et. al., *The Eucharist of the Early Christians*, trans. Matthew O'Connell (New York: Pueblo, 1978). This work contains descriptions of the eucharist from the *Didache* through the *Apostolic Constitutions* and helpful commentaries.

93. See the 1983 edition of *Pastoral Care of the Sick: Rites of Anointing and Viaticum*, noting in particular the distinction between rites for the sick and those for the dying as well as the new Mass formula in the Sacramentary if either the rite of anointing, viaticum, or both, take place during Mass.

94. The rite presumes the distribution of communion under the forms of bread and wine even when viaticum is given outside of Mass (nn. 193, 207).

95. See, for example, *General Instruction of the Roman Missal* (nn. 281–285) about bread and wine for the eucharist.

96. See Don Saliers, "Liturgical Aesthetics," in *New Dictionary of Sacramental Worship*, ed. Peter E. Fink (Collegeville: The Liturgical Press, 1990), 80–89.

97. See Pelagio Visentin, "Creazione—Storia della salvezza—liturgia," *Rivista Liturgica* 77(3): 267.

98. One of the premises of the document from the (American) Bishops' Committee on the Liturgy, *Environment and Art in Catholic Worship*, is this authenticity in sign and symbolic interaction in liturgy; see nn. 12–26 for some theoretical grounding for the document.

99. John Paul II addresses this point in "Peace with God the Creator, Peace with All of Creation: Message of His Holiness Pope John Paul II for the celebration of the World Day of Peace, 1 January, 1990" *Origins* 19(28): Nn. 14–16:

> Finally, the aesthetic value of creation cannot be overlooked. Our very contact with nature has a deep restorative power; contemplation of its magnificence imparts peace and serenity. The Bible speaks again and again of the goodness and beauty of creation, which is called to glorify God (cf. Genesis 1:4ff.; Psalm 8:2; 104:1ff.; Wisdom 13:3–5; Sirach 39:16, 33; 43:1, 9). More difficult perhaps, but no less profound, is the contemplation of the works of human ingenuity. Even cities can have a beauty all their own, one that ought to motivate people to care for their surroundings. Good urban planning is an important part of environmental protection, and respect for the natural contours of the land is an indispensable prerequisite for ecologically sound development. The relationship between a good aesthetic education and the maintenance of a healthy environment cannot be overlooked.

100. See Denis Carroll, "Creation," in *New Dictionary of Theology*, 249. Carroll states that "the Eastern conception of Christ's universal rule—Christ the Pantocrator or Cosmocrator—has much to offer this reconstruction."

101. Taken from the commentary on the *Rule* entitled "The Abbot," in *RB80: The Rule of St. Benedict in Latin and English with Notes*, ed. Timothy Fry, et.al. (Collegeville: The Liturgical Press, 1981), 370. A contemporary perspective on how the Catholic approach to the sacramentality of life can influence both sacramental and liturgical theology is offered by Philip J. Murnion, "A Sacramental Church in the Modern World," in *Origins* 14(6). Particularly notable is Murnion's call for "Benedictine-like" communities that can reflect a new order for the world based on the principle of the sacramentality in all of life. He states: [Central to any notion of sacramentality is the fact of and a belief in the incarnation. We believe that in and through Christ there is a permanent union of God and this world, the divine and the human condition. We cannot look at the special actions we call the sacraments or the particular challenges faced by the Church as sacrament without considering the present state of our world and our human condition, which are the flesh of God's presence among us.

> . . . The new order is one that recognizes explicitly, not begrudgingly, the community of all life, the interdependence of all persons, the symbiosis of human life and the environment. It also rewards relationships rather than acquisitions as the measure of success.

102. See Paul Weigand, "Escape from the Birdbath: A Reinterpretation of St. Francis as a Model for the Ecological Movement," in P. N. Joranson, ed., *Cry of the Environment*, 148–57.

103. Apostolic Letter *Inter sanctos*: Acta apostolicae sedis 71(16): 1509f.

104. John Paul II, Peace with God the Creator.

105. Some indications of the similarities and differences between these two traditions as they bear on reverence for creation are found in René

Dubois, "Franciscan Conservation Versus Benedictine Stewardship," in *Ecology and religion in history*, ed. David Spring and Eileen Spring (New York: Harper and Row, 1975), 114–36.

106. For a critique that in the reformed liturgy, liturgical scholars did not concern themselves with creation despite the fact that it was present so strongly in patristic writings about Sunday and also in oriental liturgies, see Yves M. Congar, "Le thème de Dieu-Créateur et les explications de l'hexamèrons dans la tradition chrétienne," in *L'Homme devant Dieu* 1 (Lyons: Editions Montaigne Aubiere, 1963), 189–215.

107. See Annibale Bugnini, *The Reform of the Liturgy, 1948-1975*, trans. Matthew J. O'Connell (Collegeville: The Liturgical Press, 1990), 337–92; Frederick R. McManus, "The Roman order of Mass from 1964–1969: The preparation of the gifts," *Shaping English Liturgy*, ed. Peter Finn and James Schellman (Washington: Pastoral Press, 1990), 107–38; Thomas A. Krosnicki, "Preparing the gifts: Clarifying the rite," *Worship* 65(2): 149–59; and Edward Foley, Kathleen Hughes, and Gilbert Ostdiek, "The Preparatory Rites: A Case Study in Liturgical Ecology," *Worship* 67(1): 17–38.

108. In a publication prepared by the churches participating in the Inter-Lutheran Commission on Worship, *Lutheran Book of Worship* (Minneapolis: Augsburg Publishing House, 1978), 66.

DANIEL M. COWDIN

Toward an Environmental Ethic

One of the penalties of an ecological education is that one lives alone in a world of wounds.

ALDO LEOPOLD, *A Sand County Almanac*

If God's purposes are for the well-being of the whole of "the creation," what is the place of human well-being in relation to the "whole of creation"? Man, the measurer, can no longer be the measure of the value of all things. What is right for man has to be determined in relation to man's place in the universe and, indeed, in relation to the will of God for all things as that might dimly be discerned.

JAMES GUSTAFSON, *Ethics from a Theocentric Perspective*

The task of this paper is to lay the groundwork for developing an environmental ethic through the Roman Catholic tradition. In what follows, I will not attempt to construct such an ethic but (1) to address why we ought to be seeking to construct one in the first place and (2) to reflect on what it might entail, that is, to discuss what such an ethic might look like, how it would interact with current moral theology, and what methodological options we may have for its construction. Before we can start, however, we need some understanding of what an environmental ethic is and why it is called for today. As is often the case in such issues, the church is not leading the way but seeking to legitimize, appropriate, and refine cultural and philosophical trends originating outside itself.[1] In this instance at least, things are as they should be; there ought to be no embarrassment or insecurity about the issue. There is no "environmental ethic" simply waiting to be drawn forth from scripture or tradition. An environmental ethic, rooted as it must be in ecology and evolutionary understanding and responding to dangers of unparalleled proportions, is a new thing under the sun.

Though certainly drawing on elements from the past, it is historically situated in the now. Moreover, like other areas of social ethics, its casuistry must involve knowledge of philosophy and applied sciences; thus, it will necessarily be a cross-disciplinary pursuit.

So the task of forging a Catholic environmental ethic is in part to bring together external wisdom with our own; we are not merely moving forward with an internal development. How a Catholic moral perspective may transform, and be transformed by, an "environmental ethics" will be explored later. For now, it is enough to note that when we refer to "environmental ethics," we are referring to a philosophical notion that has developed over the past forty years on its own terms; we cannot simply define the term for ourselves.

The lineage of environmental ethics begins with Aldo Leopold's "land ethic." Leopold, a sportsman, wildlife manager and conservation biologist, believed that our understanding of ethics needed to evolve beyond concern for individuals and human society to the land itself. "The extension of ethics to this third element . . . is, if I read the evidence correctly, an evolutionary possibility and an ecological necessity."[2] What has to be transcended is the evaluation of all land-use in merely economic terms; we ought as well to consider the health of the land itself. Leopold articulated it this way: "A thing is right when it tends to preserve the integrity, stability and beauty of the biotic community. It is wrong when it tends otherwise."[3]

Not much sustained philosophical attention was given to the land ethic, or to the ecological crisis generally, until the mid-seventies. John Passmore's *Man's Responsibility for Nature* treated the issue in a philosophically sophisticated but overly conservative manner. In the face of increasing environmental degradation, he argued, ecologically enlightened anthropocentrism is sufficient. "What [the West] needs, for the most part, is not so much a 'new ethic' as a more general adherence to a perfectly familiar ethic."[4] His philosophical domestication of the issue earned him the label of an ecological "Uncle Tom," and those who sought a nonanthropocentric approach set themselves against him.

Over the past fifteen years or so, a flurry of philosophical approaches arguing for varying sorts of nonanthropocentric environmental ethics have been put forward.[5] Some focus on other nonhuman organisms and argue that moral concern can be extended beyond the human community according to a characteristic (or characteristics) that humans already possess in greater abundance or intensity such as richness of life-experience.[6] Others take essentially the same route but focus on a characteristic that all species, including humans, share equally such as life itself or the possession of a telos. A less hierarchical more egalitarian framework is thus developed.[7] Still others, in the tradition of Leopold, focus not primarily on other organisms but on the natural systems, populations, and relationships within which we all function. Their approach is more holistic and can be divided into strong or weak holism. Strong holists contend that the essential center of value is the natural system to which we belong and that all individual value derives from the system as a Whole.[8] Weak holists, on the other hand, recognize systemic value but refrain from ultimately placing all individual value, particularly human value, in its service.[9]

What seems to be minimally held by all environmental ethicists, however, is the notion that our relationship to nonhuman nature considered in itself, is subject to ethical evaluation: it can be judged as right or wrong, good or bad, without further reference to human interests. As Holmes Rolston articulates it: "Environmental ethics in the *primary*, naturalistic sense is reached only when humans ask questions not merely of prudential use but of appropriate respect and duty."[10]

The ethical issue then is not how we are affected by nonhuman nature, but how it is affected by us. The assumptions behind it are that (1) we have agency vis-à-vis nonhuman nature, that is to say, some knowledge of how our actions will affect it and the freedom to act on that knowledge, and (2) we value qualities in nonhuman nature that ought to be taken into account in our action (or inaction) toward it. If either of these assumptions falls through—if we really have no idea how we affect nonhuman nature or if we are unable to value its qualities intrinsically—then we either lose our accountability for our actions or reduce our judgment of them to anthropocentric self-interest. In either case the notion of an *environmental ethic* unravels as our relationship to nonhuman nature, viewed in itself, ceases to matter in any ethical sense.

Now within this formal definition there is room for drastic variation. Nothing here is said about how much our relationship to nature,[11] considered in itself, should matter, nor about how to explain why it matters (for example because we are all evolutionary kin or biotic equals or because nature has integrities worthy of respect or because nonhumans have spirits or because God loves the nonhuman world, and so forth). What all seem to agree on, however, is that without at least some sense of our agency within nature and some sense of its intrinsic valuation, we no longer have an identifiable environmental ethic.

Intrinsic valuation raises thorny philosophical issues, such as whether value can exist independent of a valuer. This type of question is especially threatening to environmental ethics, for if all valuation is human-based then all ethics seems irreducibly anthropocentric, and environmental ethics in the sense described never gets off the ground.

One way of responding to this is to meet the challenge head-on, that is, to argue for objective natural values independent of human valuers.[12] Even if that approach fails, however, the project can still be saved by distinguishing between value (noun) and valuing (verb). Whether or not values exist "out there," it is still perfectly intelligible to distinguish between valuing nature instrumentally and valuing it intrinsically.[13] The issue can then be reframed as whether intrinsic evaluative behavior is appropriate on our part in response to nonhuman nature.[14] The question whether any value would exist if humans exited the planet thus ceases to threaten the project.

The assumption in this paper is that some version of intrinsic valuation of nature is defensible on philosophical grounds. But even if this were not the case, we could still move forward. A Catholic environmental ethic will appeal to God as valuer of nature and will thus have a resource for attributing intrinsic value to it independently of mere human valuation.

Whether our actions toward nature matter in a moral sense has become more than an issue of imaginative philosophical and theological speculation. We are at a new moment in the history of our planet. We are at a moment when human history—the story of our cultural self-construction—and natural history—the story of the eco-evolutionary construction of life in the world—intersect in a manner previously unknown. We are at a point at which these histories unite in a definitive manner through human consciousness, and the basic direction of eco-evolutionary history becomes partially, but really, our cultural responsibility. The flow of life is in our hands.

The newness of the moment is not the interconnection between these two histories per se. Our species history is, of course, a product of natural history though the way and extent to which it is has only recently come to light. What makes this a genuinely new and decisive moment in world history is not primarily the realization of our dependence on nature but the fact and realization of nature's dependence on us.

What this fragile "blue planet" looks like in the next 22,000 or 2 million years is directly dependent on how we organize ourselves in this generation. It is the stunning yet undeniable facticity of this power relationship that puts us into a position of "lordship" or "dominion," such as it is, and makes the issue of the moral dimensions of this power one of practical urgency. We as a species are faced with (have created for ourselves) a choice of global proportions. Never before has nature on a planetary scale been our self-conscious task. We have, to use Bonhoeffer's oft-quoted phrase, "come of age"—not merely with respect to social and political self-determination but with respect to the entire planet. Like it or not, it is partially but really in our hands, and we are responsible for what happens next. Whether that responsibility should be understood morally is the question we now face.

I will argue in what follows that the Catholic Church can and ought to add its moral voice to this *kairos* by developing its own grounds for an environmental ethic. In the first section of the paper, I will articulate a "fundamental option" for nature at the deepest level as well as briefly discuss a parallel articulation using natural law language. An environmental ethic cannot be "added on" to the tradition in a supplementary way, however. Whatever the specifics, the entrance of an environmental ethic into the Catholic moral tradition will reverberate through the tradition and force readjustments, particularly in our understanding of human dignity. I will therefore discuss this transformation in the second part of the paper and indicate a line of thinking that can expand our sense of human dignity without sacrificing the gains we have already made in that concept. I will in the third section address methodological issues and various options for the shape of an environmental ethic. Its specifics are up for debate, and it is not my purpose to address them in any full-blown way. I will indicate certain general directions and criticize others that seem vulnerable. My point is not to resolve the debate but to open it. I will conclude with some thoughts on nature and eschatology.

A FUNDAMENTAL OPTION FOR NATURE?

A Confusion of Intuitions

Why value nonhuman nature intrinsically? Why act in light of those values? The answers are not self-evident, and there is even a counter-cultural bizarreness to the idea that positive answers can be given. We must refashion our concepts philosophically and theologically in order to generate adequate responses.

At the same time there is something shocking about having to go through this process at all on such a basic level, building an environmental ethic from the ground up. The idea that the argumentative presumption lies with those who envision no more significance to our relationship with nature than self-interested instrumentality seems unnatural. Do we really have to justify being pro-life in such a basic sense?

We are in the strange position then of sensing that both the need for the questions and the possible answers provided are counterintuitive. The burden of argument seems misplaced, but the attempts to meet the burden—to articulate the basis for respecting nature in an ethical sense—seem awkward and unsatisfactory. Why?

The first reason lies in the unique depth of our relationship to nature. Our relationship to nature is so vast, so deep, so given, so multifaceted, so complicated, that the attempt to affirm it at a foundational level seems awkward, trite, inadequate. It is like a long-married couple, or a parent and child, being asked to articulate what they mean to each other after thirty-five years of relationship. There is a self-evidence to the depth of the bond, rooted in the reality of the relationship itself, that makes all such attempts to reduce it to words seem shallow. Indeed, there is even a sense in which having to do so is an affront, as though we had missed the quality of the relationship from the start. Similarly with our relationship to nature. To make its protection depend on whether we can satisfactorily articulate its value is to miss the depth of our relationship to it. To have the burden of justifying our opposition to the destruction of vast components of nature within which we have always lived seems ludicrous. The burden should be on the other side.

This affront is not a strategic dodge. Articulating the meaning of our relationship to nature is crucial as it is with all relationships of depth. But believing that its significance hinges on whether it can be expressed in our current moral vocabulary is inappropriate. The task is best seen as one of exploring ways to articulate a significance that is assumed already to exist, rather than assuming that no such depth exists unless the words immediately disclose it. And this will involve some experimentation with moral language. In order to gain room for such experimentation though, the burden of argument needs to be shifted to those who believe that exploitation, even enlightened, is the sum of our relationship to nature.

A second reason for a confusion of intuitions lies in the fact that at least one dimension of our relationship to nature must be conflictual. Like other species, we do not arrive on this planet with our home ready-made; rather we need to make our niche through active, often violent, interaction with our surroundings. Moreover, in addition to the normal conflict with our surroundings that all species share, we need to build niches insulated from nature itself. We find no niche in nature per se; instead we build cultures in which a whole new set of formative factors—symbols, ideas, economics, and politics, for example—take on a life and integrity of their own and impact our identities. Culture can only be accomplished, however, insofar as nature is conquered, channeled, transformed, or harnessed for our purposes. In short, we do what we need to do to survive, and to survive as humans, in cultures. We are thus twice-distanced from nature.

As we begin to articulate why nature should be treated morally, something counterintuitive seems to be taking place. Are we projecting on to nature standards of meaning and behavior appropriate only within human culture? We do not need to exploit other humans—when we do so, we have failed either in moral will or moral imagination, or both. But we do need to exploit nature constantly even if only partially. Why then see the relationship in ethical terms?

This question is an understandable, and crucial, challenge to our project. It is not to be taken lightly. Any adequate ethic will do more than dodge the element of conflict with, and alienation from, nature, as though it were merely an unfortunate blip on the screen of eco-evolutionary mutuality. A comprehensive ethic will do more than simply allow for it as a regrettable necessity. Rather, this relationship needs to be understood and organically grounded in the ethic from the start.[15] An environmental ethic cannot, if it is to do justice to our actual relationship to nature, be rooted solely in preservationist nonintervention. But neither do we do justice to it by portraying it in purely instrumental terms.

Our most basic relationship to nature is conflictual; but that does not mean that conflict is our only, or even our most fully human, form of interaction. We have historically almost always related to nature in a more than instrumental sense. Genesis recognizes nature as good, and the psalms glory in its wonders. Countless examples of aesthetic and religious valuation of nature abound through history and across cultures. In the past, the intrinsic valuation of nature could coexist with its resourceful exploitation because the latter rarely threatened the former. There was not much that we could do to nature in any final or definitive way. Nature was seemingly vast and unconquerable, impacting us with its own regularities over which we had little control. Its resources seemed infinitely plentiful, unable to be used up. To take a rather recent and familiar example: Daniel Boone could be conceived at one and the same time as a nature-lover and as nature's conqueror. The two were not in contradiction so long as there was always a frontier, a never-ending supply of nature "out there."[16] In such (perceived) circumstances, our use of nature and our appreciation of it could coexist without contradiction, and our intrinsic valuation of it remained largely an aesthetic, not ethical, matter.

Technology of course has changed all this and in so doing has given our intrinsic valuation an ethical dimension: the things we appreciate in nature can be forever altered, warped, and even extinguished by us. These natural values now become something that we have to defend rather than something we can enjoy; in short, we can no longer take them for granted. Today we are in a zero-sum game: we are in a position of losing what we value intrinsically because we are abusing it instrumentally.

The move from the intrinsic valuation of nature to defending those values when they are put into jeopardy seems not that radical a jump, though the task of coherently integrating this defense with our other relationships to nature is formidable. Granting that our instrumental use of nature precedes all others (we need to survive to appreciate), this does not make our intrinsic appreciation of it unintelligible, trivial, or any less urgent in this time when nature is so drastically at our mercy. It is true that we cannot simply treat nature like we treat each other; but it is also true that we cannot go on treating nature like a mere "thing" and expect it to be with us in its present form much longer. Our necessarily conflictual relationship with nature makes this a different task than intrahuman morality—particularly at the level of the universalization of principles—but it is not for that reason any less moral.[17]

Thus, we face a real question about how to conceptualize such an ethic and an urgency to complete the task. The sheer depth of our relationship to nature, as well as its necessarily conflictual element, lend an air of awkwardness and complexity to the project; but I have tried to argue that these countervailing intuitions need not, and ought not, foreclose it. Indeed the burden of argument should be on those who would think otherwise.

And yet in the industrialized West, it is only recently that the burden has begun to shift to its proper place. Not too long ago, acting as if nature mattered intrinsically was portrayed as foreign and bizarre by the reigning cultural ethos. We had reached a point in our cultural history when we were less than confused: we had simply reduced nature to the single dimension of human utility. People who questioned that reduction were seen as on the fringe. Many who in fact did have richer experiences in nature (such as hunters, fishers, and vacationers) had to smuggle them into cultural acceptance under the guise of "resource use."

There is something particular to the recent experience of the industrialized West that intensifies the suspicion against an environmental ethic over and above the countervailing intuitions we have already explored. Even more so the burden is really on those who would defend such an outlook as the norm rather than an aberration of human history. It is a burden I doubt they can meet.

Cultural Contradictions

Our culture is sick. Our modern scientific, postindustrial, urbanized, technological existence alienates us from nature in a peculiarly drastic way relative to other stages in human history. Our sense of meaningless contingency in an accidental process, joined with our sense of power over nature, as well as an urban life style that literally requires a self-conscious effort on our part to sense any connection with nature at all—these factors enhance our sense of separateness from the natural world in a historically unparalleled way. Nature becomes for us alternately cold and indifferent, a source for giddy hubris or simply irrelevant to the stuff of day-to-day life. We become alternately cigarette-smoking existentialists, techno-brats, or experiential aliens on our own planet. Whatever the case, nature's intrinsic value becomes hard to see, feel, or touch, much less conceptualize and defend ethically.

Our felt-experience of nature has atrophied on a mass scale. No wonder then that we behave *en masse* and habitually as if nature did not exist. Indeed a huge portion of our ecological degradation is not the result of being self-consciously "at war" with nature, battling it for our own survival and cultural richness. To be honest: a vast proportion of it stems from a reckless disregard for nature, from a sense that it just does not matter what we do to it or simply from its absence from our consciousness. The impact of our daily urban actions on nature is cut off from our awareness (though this is changing for the better).

And yet on the other hand, this extremely alienating set of factors has resulted in a reaction on a mass scale toward the other extreme. We flee our techno-urban life style in exodus toward wilderness areas and national parks. The "nature experience"—and here I mean nature in a rather pristine, untrammeled sense—takes on a therapeutic role (witness the film *The Grand Canyon*, for example). This cultural phenomenon is a relatively new thing under the sun, often approaching (and reaching) religious proportions.[18] Our relationship to nature not only becomes expanded but idealized and romanticized. We are learning not only to appreciate it but to need it in its wild state; and not only to need it but also to love it.

And so we are polarized. In the city, we live as though nature hardly exists, exploiting it and dumping on it with an astounding casualness given the radical love we have for its pristine splendor when we are away from the city at other times of the year. It is almost as if we lived in two kingdoms, without understanding the facts or the ethical dimensions to their interrelationship. This poses a special problem for our task: our philosophical and political options tend to lurch between thoughtless exploitation and radical preservation, between nature as exploitable and nature as untouchable. Our relationship to nature was previously integrated through our primarily agricultural life style, which involved both respect for and use of nature.[19] Since the vast majority of us no longer have access to that life style, one of the tasks of a religiously based ethic is to overcome this radical polarization on other levels (theology and liturgy, for example) so that our relationship to nature does not simply fracture into irreconcilable parts. We need to overcome the alienation of the urban mentality without laying our entire ethical foundation on the experience of pristine nature.[20]

The drastic alienation of modern scientific, technological, urban life from nature is a peculiar cultural sickness; it needs to be dismantled for the illusion that it is or at least cured of its myopia. The currently popular communion with pristine wilderness—which is not merely a reaction to but a creation of modern scientific, technological life—should be embraced for the epiphany it has given us on a mass scale.[21] But the cure of the former cannot take place solely through the medicine of the latter: it is pragmatically implausible and dubious philosophically. Viewing nature in purely nonexploitative terms is as myopic as viewing it in purely instrumental ones. Indeed the extremely polarized cycle of migration between the two (both in thought and action) reveals a lack of balance in our relationship to nature.

We ought not merely replicate this lived-polarization on a philosophical and theological level; we ought rather to work toward healing it. We need to make sense of, protect, yet coherently integrate, our multiple relationships to nature, not simply idealize one over another. This idea is fortuitous perhaps for a Catholic approach: as a tradition with an already existing rationale for transforming nature, as well as a tendency toward synthesis rather than polarization, we have a unique opportunity to achieve comprehensiveness. Perhaps it can be a distinctively Catholic contribution to the task.

Re-envisioning Our Relationship to Nature

Beginning at the Beginning: Nature as Real: We can start by reminding ourselves that nature is real—an absurdly basic, banal point for an absurdly alienated culture, but a basic we need to get back to and relearn how to feel. Lodged at the heart of Trinitarian self-understanding is the belief in all that is seen in God's creation as real. It does exist, and for us to live otherwise is, in Christian terms, to have lost touch with reality. We are at this cultural moment in the West, living a lie: the lie that human culture is simply self-enclosed and self-sufficient. Every time we act with reckless disregard for the larger ecological impact of our actions we live in self-delusion. We need somehow to reestablish our perception of nature as real and not finally detached from our daily urban lives (as though nature only existed in parks and preserves).

Nature as Constitutive: Nature is not only real, it is constitutive of who we are. We literally do not know ourselves if we take nature out of the picture. Our very identity as a species is dependent on the natural processes out of which we have emerged and in response to which we have forged ourselves. We are as Holmes Rolston puts it, "environmental reciprocals, indebted to our environment for what we have become in ways that are as complementary as they are oppositional."[22]

What we have lost, at the deepest level, is a sense of being in fundamental relationship to the earth. Thus, the first thing to put back in place is not any single dimension of our relationship but the relationship per se. We need to reestablish, in thought and feeling, the experience of the earth as real and as inextricably part of who we are. We need to dislodge the experience of nature as an unnecessary prop for the "real" task of our existence as humans. We are in an inevitable relationship to nature; we are, in short, embodied. But we are also more than that: we are not just constituted by our bodies, for our bodies are constituted by our history in nature. We are embodied and *enmeshed* in the larger natural environment. Excusing the neologism, we are one might say, im-planeted.

Western religions have been notoriously unhelpful here, especially Christianity. Catholicism is somewhat of an exception and has been criticized by other Christian traditions for being so. The deepest problem Christianity poses for the environment I believe, is not its deanimation of nature nor its call to dominion, but its tendency to believe that ultimately our relationship to nature does not matter. It is not legitimizing the transformation of nature that is finally the most dangerous thing, but doing so with a sense of nature's final irrelevance to distinctively human meaning. For this reason I think Paul Santmire is correct to focus on the issue of whether nature can be part of the "fundamental data" of theology, a "given in the original moment of theological reflection" along with God and humanity.[23] And his answer—that it has been and can be—is correct I believe.

Our relationship to nature cannot be exhaustively summed up by any one interrelation, be it opposition, exploitation, transformation, understanding, appreciation, or nurturance. The point of saying that nature is constitutive is to look more deeply for the connection underlying all these relationships. To return to an earlier analogy, we might say that our modern predicament is as if the earth woke up one morning and discovered we had filed for a divorce. For most of our species history, the world has simply been a part of who we are, an assumed partner, not so much irrelevant as taken for granted, a place of conflict and appreciation, of sustenance and trial, of sustenance through trial. And the current task is to maintain it as such, if we can.

Making a Fundamental Option: Nature as Good: Once we have reinstituted a sense of nature as real (we have actually gone some distance toward doing so already) and moreover as a constitutive part of who we are, we can try to move forward to an articulation of nature as basically good. Part of its goodness will be its goodness for us, but in an overarching sense we will try to say that nature is good in itself. We want to be able to see in the flow of natural history and the existence of the various biotic communities and life-forms with us that "it is good" at the most basic level. This goodness is the basic cornerstone of an environmental ethic because it stands in direct opposition to the idea that nature does not matter or that it is somehow, when all is said and done, our enemy.

The next step is to link that fundamental perception to a fundamental practical attitude and thus make a fundamental option: as nature is good at the most basic level we must choose to be *for* nature at our most basic level of human orientation toward the world. Richard Gula describes a fundamental option as

A choice which arises from such a personal depth that it can significantly reverse or reinforce the fundamental direction of our lives. . . . To qualify as a fundamental option, a choice must be rooted in a deep knowledge of self and a freedom to commit oneself. Through a fundamental option we express our basic freedom of self-determination to commit ourselves profoundly toward a certain way of being in the world.[24]

Although there are philosophical difficulties with transferring such a notion to the corporate level of church, nation, or species, surely a tradition rooted in covenant as we are can at least allow for it analogically. As a species we have a radically new understanding of ourselves as products of the eco-evolutionary process; we have the freedom to commit ourselves to a far less ecologically damaging life style; we understand with new eyes the fragile wonder of this life-system. In short, we have a new appreciation of our connection to this earth and its intrinsic goodness, and we have the capacity to act on it. We thus have the corporate requisites "to commit ourselves profoundly toward a certain way of being in the world," a way of being profoundly at odds with our current one. We ought to opt to live with and in this world, not merely next to or on top of it. And this means not destroying vast portions of it in the process.

It is important not to lose sight of the fact that this is an option. It is a profoundly human capacity to be able to see something as real, even basic to one's identity, and still reject it in some ultimate sense. Indeed one could argue that the monotheistic religious impulse, at its core, depends on exactly this capacity. Minimally, the reality of such a choice is the basis of our agency, of our moral imagination and the freedom to act in light of it over against the status quo. Whether to acquiesce to the givens of nature or to fight them (and how to do so in either case) is one way of articulating the fundamental question of morality.

An environmental ethic thus puts us back on old ground but in a new way. The choice here is not whether to acquiesce to brute nature or battle it but whether to make a self-conscious decision to fit into its basic directionality and order. This choice demands neither total submission to, nor total rejection of, nature as it is but creative adaptation. To adapt to the flow and integrity of nature as we perceive it is to opt, at a fundamental level, for nature; to remain indifferent to or work against that flow and integrity is to opt against it.

I am not arguing that it is self-evidently clear that we should opt for nature in this sense. There are warrants for opting against it. The natural system seems arbitrary, undirected, with no particular telos; its mechanisms are violent and seemingly wasteful; its appropriateness for us at times seems questionable as we forge our civilizations against the generally inhospitable natural surroundings in which we apparently have no real niche. We can imagine a better set-up, both generally and for us in particular.

Yet the question at hand is how we act toward this set-up, not an imaginary one. This is the only world we have and the only life-producing planetary system we know. Why sacrifice the real for the imaginary? Our world need not be perfect to be valuable and worth protecting.

Moreover the moral imagination can work for our fundamental option as well as against it. Imagine that we discover life on other planets much simpler than our own; what would our response likely be? Almost certainly it would be one of awe, wonder, and perhaps even reverence. To destroy that life arbitrarily, by using the planets for nuclear waste, for example, would be greeted as an attitude bordering on the insane. Why then do we think we can opt to reject life here?

> If a space probe were to find on Mars life of the complexity of the Yellowstone thermophiles, to say nothing of those lousewarts and snail darters, it would be the most epochal discovery in the history of science and we would value there what is daily despised on Earth.[25]

Further, in spite of our lack of niche, we have as a species developed tools to overcome this lack—tools to make the entire earth our niche. This development has taken time—we have our own story of forging this planetary niche—but it has been accomplished nevertheless. We do not fit instinctively, but we can fit self-consciously. And if we do not beg the question by categorizing these "tools" as unnatural; that is, if we see our distinctively human capacities as evolutionary products emergent from the system, then it is hard to say that we are not equipped by nature to be here.

Although the notion of evolution toward a particular telos of some sort is unsubstantiated, the scientific record does not preclude perceiving an important directionality to the sweep of natural history. In particular the life-process seems to tend toward greater complexity and diversity over time, or what has been termed "species-packing."[26] The general flow of evolution is toward more and more kinds of life existing at more and more complex levels of being, a flow interrupted only by apparently aberrant moments of "catastrophic extinction." Thus, "natural history—a sometimes despised term . . . has an epic quality, a certain wandering not withstanding."[27] The question for us is this: what part in this epic story do we want to play? Ought we to induce yet another catastrophic extinction, or rather try to fit in with the directional pro-life and pro-quality-of-life, flow (of which we are the most recent amazing product)?

In the end it is "not death but life, including human life fitted to this planetary environment, [that] is the principal mystery that has come out of nature."[28] This stance is neither unreasonable nor unrealistically optimistic. Life, expanding and diversifying, eventually self-conscious and ultimately moral and valuational, is the principal mystery; to be for it at a most basic level seems right at a most basic level.

Whether, in the end, all this is a loving mystery or an isolated mystery destined to burn out into nothingness, is not finally resolvable short of faith. The heroism of someone like Bertrand Russell, however, standing freely against nature because of its arbitrariness and eventual finality, seems arbitrarily anthropocentric in its outlook.[29] Why pit human beings against nature in response to the coldness of the universe? Why not stand out with all life against the tides of chaos and nothingness, even if such bleak heroism is the only option? Why not fight with and for nature against entropy? The enemy is not the natural system but the empty inertness that engulfs it on all sides.

It is thus warranted, though not certainly, for us to make a fundamental option for nature, to basically come to terms with this world and ourselves as belonging within it, to trust the world enough to try and fit into it in some basic sense, to go its way. Within a Catholic framework, the fundamental stance for nature becomes more than a reasonable option: it becomes an imperative.

Existence itself is good. A steadily increasing richness of existence is even better. We have said that before in the Catholic tradition, and often it seems the ethereal abstraction of scholastic philosophy; in our context, however, when a great deal of existence is in human hands, when we can turn the planet into another lifeless orb, the affirmation takes on practical import. To snuff out the natural process, or even to threaten it, is arbitrarily antilife and an assault on God's purposes as we perceive them.

That nature is good is open to dispute. It is paradigmatically Catholic, however, to be open to the dispute and simultaneously to have faith that the dispute is ultimately resolvable on the side of life as we know it. We believe that emptiness is not the final engulfing reality, but we have the courage to face the world as it presents itself to us in the process of living that belief. This attitude says to me that the basic Catholic religious ethos propels us both toward trying to forge an ethic and toward trying to do so honestly, based on accessible reasons open to argumentation.

Although I have been using the modern language of fundamental option, another way of understanding our task at this level is in terms of a basic principle of natural law. In Thomistic language, the moral task was for us to participate in God's eternal law through our own reason and freedom. At the most basic level we were meant to perceive the basic directionality of our species-being and rationally to get in step with it. Specifically, for Aquinas, it meant three things: affirming and organizing our orientation toward survival, procreation, and life in community.[30] As the modern reappropriation of Thomas has shown, such an understanding of natural law was neither legalistic nor physicalist.[31] The foundational precepts were not concrete rules asking us simply to conform to the physical givens of life; rather, they were general imperatives to self-consciously, humanly, join up with those givens in a rationally creative manner.

But today we understand on both scientific and scriptural grounds that all of nature does not exist for human nature. God's purposes in creation, such as we can glean them, do not seem limited to human flourishing. The world is not in any way ready-made just for us but is a multiplicity of systems and life-forms, exceeding us in a vast way, interacting and evolving, all of which God deems good. Thus as Job learns, the entire planet does not turn on the axis of our moral-soteriological drama. Other things are going on.

If this is true then participating in the eternal law must involve more than getting in step with who we are as a species; it must include taking on the mind of God, such as we can, with regard to the rest of the planet as well. And the mind of God seems to value other life-forms and the whole process, as good in a basic and fundamental way, not merely as instrumental for us. Our own perceptions of natural history, ecosystems, species, and other living beings resonates with this.

The eternal law then seems not to be exhaustively concerned with human interests; nor should we be, if we want to participate in it. To participate in the eternal law is not only to cultivate our own flourishing, but minimally not to swim against the stream of the increasing diversity and complexity of natural history. Should we not add, therefore, a new precept to the natural law? Something like: respect the flow of life, its systemic integrity and other life-forms; survive, reproduce, and form societies *within* the overarching framework of an ever-expanding life-flow, not at its expense.

Let us say that this, or something close to it, is the fourth precept of the natural law (in addition to the formal principle of doing good and avoiding evil). It rests, like the others, on the idea that what is right and good is intertwined with the way the world is and thus that the world can and ought to be trusted. And it functions like the others at a high level of generality, orienting us in a fundamental way toward ourselves and our surroundings. It rules out orientations and even behaviors that stand in direct opposition to it (such as intentionally or arbitrarily or thoughtlessly damaging nonhuman nature or damaging it so drastically that its very integrity as a life-producing system is threatened), and it leaves much to be decided about how it should be accomplished. This precept is the concrete, historical human task. Unlike the others, however, it has a nonhuman focus and thus ethically enmeshes humanity in a context beyond itself. The goods of human and nonhuman creation are organically, not merely instrumentally, intertwined. The impact of this will place new limits on human actions, but expand what it means to be human; for it implies that part of what it is to be fully human is to be able to value and act with respect for nonhuman creation.

Why Pursue an Environmental Ethic?

Nature exists. It is real. It exists beyond human being and is not merely subsumable or tributary to it, in fact or in value. We are dependent on nature for our survival and for the richness of our life. It is part of who we are as human beings, not only of our origins but of our present identity and who we will and should become. Nature is good in itself though not in an unqualified way. And, I will add at this point, we hope it is part of what our life will be as ultimately transformed by God.

We should thus pursue an environmental ethic, joining our Catholic voice to the worldwide attempt to stem the current direction of nature-exploitation before the earth is damaged beyond repair. A comprehensive ethic will involve articulating in detail the goodness of nature at various levels, learning how to balance these values among each other and against other human interests, and recognizing the political and economic dimensions of the problem. Such comprehensiveness is beyond our task here, which is simply to ground the project and indicate how best to move it along. Before doing so however, its impact on other aspects of Catholic morality, and in particular human dignity, needs to be explored.

HUMAN DIGNITY AND ENVIRONMENTAL ETHICS

Any environmental ethic worthy of the name will call us out of ourselves and demand that we place the human species within a context larger than, and to a significant degree independent of, ourselves. It will demand that we recognize that we are not the only beings that matter, nor are our cultures the only systems that matter, nor is our history the only story that matters on this planet. Nonhuman life-forms, ecosystems and biotic communities, and the flow of natural history are real and call forth a response from us beyond instrumentality. Environmental ethics pulls us out of moral solipsism, pointing to the value of the world around us.

Viewed in broad terms the task seems congenial to the tradition as a whole. Catholicism has a long history of both taking moral agency seriously while placing it within the larger context of the world around us. This history rests on a deeper foundation of affirming the importance of God as Creator, the essential goodness of creation (even after the fall), and the ultimate appropriateness of embodied existence. In a general sense, an environmental ethic should come "naturally" for Catholicism, not merely in light of Thomism but in light of our high sacramentality, our tendency to take the world seriously on a theological level, and, for example, the Franciscan strand in our tradition.

Yet recent Catholic moral thought—and the theology underlying it—has been dominated by notions of subjective personhood, so much so that it is often climactically proclaimed that the beginning and end of all morality, be it social or interpersonal, is the human person understood as subject. Timothy O'Connell for example, writes:

> For morality, after all, is *nothing else* than the responsibility that follows from the intrinsic dignity of human persons, the responsibility of human persons to be caretakers to themselves and one another. Therefore to "dispose" of a human person is to cut the very legs out from under the moral enterprise . . . human persons are not objects next to other objects, to be relatively compared in the process of resolving value conflicts. Rather, human persons are subjects, on whom the very existence of the moral enterprise is built.[32]

Similarly the social ethics tradition seems grounded in exclusively anthropocentric terms. David Hollenbach writes:

The fundamental and dominant concern of the tradition has been single and clear: the preservation and promotion of the dignity of the human person . . . this dignity is a characteristic of all persons—the ground from which emerge *all* moral claims, all rights, all duties.[33]

For Hollenbach as for O'Connell, the key contrast for setting human dignity into relief comes from nonhuman nature:

Finite beings in which the tensions of historicity are not present are dumb, brute, unconscious—in short, they are things. Beings in which such tensions are present are human persons. They are neither things nor pieces in a social machine.[34]

There is good reason for this current emphasis, as we all know: it counters not only the objectifying trends in twentieth-century politics and science but centuries of depersonalizing "objectivity" within the church in the form of natural law physicalism, ecclesiastical authoritarianism, and sociopolitical paternalism. The common thread—the common threat—in all these phenomena is the loss of human dignity as people are made passive objects of manipulation by the powers that be. Indeed history is given soteriological significance based on whether its institutions, technologies, and economies recognize and enhance human dignity or squelch it. As *Gaudium et spes* states, these things are "of vital concern to the kingdom of God."[35]

But with the emergence of environmental ethics at this key moment in world history a problem is posed for Catholic moral theology: can its direction be rerouted back toward the objective without threatening the crucial gains made for the human person through the turn to the subject? Can the world beyond the human person be reinvested with intrinsic value and meaning without subverting our current understanding of human dignity? Or is the only way of maintaining our sense of dignified, subjective personhood to set the rest of the world in bald, overly simplistic, indeed reductionistic contrast to it? In order for us to be dignified does the rest of the world have to be drained of moral value?

I noted in the beginning of the paper that Catholicism and environmental ethics will mutually transform each other. We are now at a point of focusing more specifically on that mutual transformation.

In current Catholic moral theology and social ethics, the recognition of genuinely moral relations with nonhuman nature cannot be merely a matter of supplementation: the standard formulation of human dignity in terms of subject versus object, that which we cannot reductively manipulate and that which we can, those whom we treat as ends versus the rest of the world that we can apparently treat as a mere means—in short, the persons versus *things* distinction—must be reworked. We exist within a continuum of life, sharing degrees of consciousness, mobility, and vitality, all produced and maintained by life-giving systems and processes. Clearly much of nonhuman nature can be valued intrinsically and thus treated as an end in some sense; what then distinguishes our treatment of each other from our treatment of nonhumans? This distinction will have to be analyzed.

If the transformation that environmental ethics induces within Catholic morality involves getting outside of and beyond the person, the reciprocal transformation that Catholicism induces within environmental ethics is to get back inside the person. The recognition of the genuinely human nature of this task has often been played down, or even denied, by environmental ethicists based on a fear of anthropocentrism. Much attention has been given to nature in itself, not much to being distinctively human in nature.[36] In a sense, any environmental ethic will have to go through the human, through what it means to be a person, in order to be an ethic at all. What is it about the person that makes an environmental ethic intelligible and normative? This question, too, will have to be addressed.

Repositioning Human Dignity: Respecting Everything

Environmental ethics indicts the crude inadequacy of conceiving the world, descriptively or morally, in terms of persons versus things. A pure thing is simply inert material, a stone, for example. But a cell can be a living thing and a plant a living organism and an animal a sentient, mobile living organism. A species is a genetic life-form persisting through individuals interacting with their environment over time, while an ecosystem is a loose community of things and organisms in some form of life-sustaining dynamic stability. Environmental ethics argues that the various qualities, integrities, and functions of all these "things" can and do make morally relevant differences with regard to how we treat them, for they can be valued intrinsically. As Kenneth Goodpaster has argued, something need not be a moral agent in order to be *morally considerable*.[37]

If this is so—if nonhuman nature is not adequately approached as so much thinghood—then the persons versus things contrast becomes misleading as a guide to understanding morality in general. Obviously ecosystems, species, and various organisms are not persons, but neither should they be treated as mere things: as merely so much stuff to be manipulated as efficiently as possible. Furthermore, this recognition makes the classic contrast inadequate as a formulation of the basic content of *human* dignity since it no longer reveals what it is about *personhood* that is specifically unique. We are not merely objects, things, and thus ought not to be treated as mere means, but nor should other members of the natural community. More needs to be disclosed about the particular way in which human persons ought to be respected as ends.

Environmental ethics makes morality multifaceted. Since we do not live amid a world of things but amid a world of life-generating processes, systems, life-forms, and organisms, we ought to take into account what the rest of the world is in deciding how to relate to it. We ought, in short, to *respect* it. To respect something means to see it for what it is and act accordingly. And this will entail a complex variety of insights and responses.

The proper way to treat human beings, to be together as humans entails a recognition and actualization of who we are as beings. This entailment is what we have traditionally called "morality." We do not share it with other life-forms or processes. It turns on personhood—on transcendental subjectivity that includes freedom and reason and the ability to love—and we make a grave moral error when we treat each other in ways not befitting it, that is, when we treat each other as we might treat an animal or a plant. When we respect each other, we respect this subjective personhood, this dignity.

There are also proper and improper ways to be with the nonhuman world. Here, too, we can respect others for what they are, and when we do so, we discover realities such as life-generation, stability, complexity, diversity, "storied achievement," beauty, spontaneity and order, to name a few.[38] We do not, need not, ought not, treat them as persons—they do not have dignity in that sense. But we ought to treat them as what they are—more to be sure than mere things.

Extending the community of moral care means respecting and responding to each being, process, or system according to what it is. The distinction between our treatment of humans and our treatment of others is not that of means versus ends, or moral versus amoral, but turns rather on the reality of what each thing is to which we are relating. Being as descriptively honest as possible with regard to our surroundings thus becomes an imperative.

Why not then make the overarching ethical imperative: respect everything for what it most fully is and treat it as far as possible in accordance with that perception. On the surface this may sound too atomistic, but it is not: by "everything" is meant both other individuals and the larger orders within which they exist such as species, ecosystems, and biotic communities. All are proper candidates for moral considerability. Moreover they interpenetrate: what any individual most fully is includes these larger contexts out of which it comes and within which it sustains itself.

Human dignity thus becomes one instance of this overarching imperative. We should treat humans as humans and not as something else; and nonhumans, be they individuals or systems, as what they are and not as something else. It is part of human dignity to respect other persons as ourselves; is it not also part of our dignity to respect nonhuman others not as ourselves but as they are? The special status of human being is therefore maintained while the real status of other life around us is not blocked from view or reduced. We can simultaneously insist on the unique demands of the human moral community without making such demands the beginning or end of all morality.

Rearticulating Human Dignity: Being Human in Nature

One source for grounding this vision is the modern scientific understanding of the human person as a unique evolutionary emergent within a continuum of other emergents. We are both deeply connected to and radically different from the wider world. Our particular way of being, our human being, is genuinely different in kind from other life-forms, though not for that reason in any sort of metaphysical discontinuity with the overall life-process of which we are a part. By emergence then is meant something qualitatively new, not a mere unfolding of what was already present; we are not reducible to other life-forms. Yet our newness is not interpretable as removing us metaphysically from the system as a whole.

An evolutionary-based vision knocks away two key assumptions in Christian thought that block the formation of an environmental ethic. The first is that nature is solely for us—ordered for our particular good as a species and fulfilled in and through our transformation of it, as though the whole enterprise were meant for us. The universe is neither statically ordered nor ordered to our particular species-needs. It is possible for us to make it our home, but the fit is not always easy. Other beings have their own stories and natures, the result of challenge and response within a changing environment. We have argued that not only is it possible to see with Job the independence of life around us but to see it as good and to try to act as such.

The second traditional assumption that evolutionary theory threatens is our fundamental ontological discontinuity with nature. We share ninety-nine percent of our genetic make-up with African gorillas, for example, and like other species, have emerged within a dynamic natural process. The underlying continuity amid the qualitative differences is not trivial. An animal differs radically from a plant as does a plant from a stone; this does not make either "unnatural" in any fundamental sense. Neither, then, should our uniqueness as self-conscious valuers—free, reasoning, religious beings—make us fundamentally unnatural.

The key is that our radical qualitative difference from the rest of nature—the uniquely human way of being—is not a participation in a metaphysically distinct dimension of reality which just happens to be awkwardly conjoined to "nature." Our distinctively human way of being is part of the one tapestry of reality known as nature. This difference is not a "reduction" of human being in any morally dangerous sense. Such a criticism is misdirected for three reasons: (1) since nature itself is no longer conceived as stolid, inert, material thinghood, inclusion within it no longer implies objectification; (2) the qualitative uniqueness of human being from other forms of being is maintained; and (3) the expectation of eschatological transformation can still hold (for us and nature as a whole).

Thus, on the level of philosophical anthropology, conceiving ourselves as evolutionary emergents supports the moral uniqueness of the human community without making unintelligible the extension of moral respect for members of the surrounding world. They are radically different from us but not so utterly foreign as to make our respect incoherent or meaningless.

Further, conceiving ourselves as unique evolutionary emergents grounds us in the challenge-response aspect of the system itself. Our opportunistic use of nature is part of our development and functioning; we need not see it as intrinsically evil per se but we can endorse it as a necessary and constructive part of being enmeshed on this planet.

Yet to indulge it recklessly with no thought to its impact is to deny our particular species-being. Humans are unique, not just in our capacity to be technological beings, nor just in our capacity to be sociopolitical, cultured beings; we are unique in our capacity to understand and value and act with respect for the rest of the planet. As Leopold once wrote on the occasion of memorializing the passenger pigeon that had been hunted to extinction:

> We, who have lost our pigeons, mourn the loss. Had the funeral been ours, the pigeons would hardly have mourned us. In this fact, rather than in Mr. Dupont's nylons or Mr. Vannevar Bush's bombs, lies objective evidence of our superiority over the beasts.[39]

Now I would contend that the issue in environmental ethics is not just that of respecting the nonhuman but in understanding the humanness of doing so. The task is not finally to deny ourselves in light of the nonhuman but to *be* ourselves amid the nonhuman. And this task entails using our capacities to the fullest, including especially those of understanding and valuing and acting with respect for nature. We are, as it is commonly said, evolution's self-consciousness. Surely this involves a receptive, valuational component—a "seventh day" (or more) of rest and appreciation.

To argue that self-serving instrumentality is the only or even paradigmatic way to interact with nature is to concede our humanity. Our task is to be *human in nature*. And that means to bring our most distinctively human capacities to bear in our interaction with it. To do nothing but exploit nature is neither a fulfillment nor a consequence of human dignity; it is an abdication of it. To say that we exhaust the reality of nature by making it serve us is once again to live a lie—but this time about ourselves.

Human dignity conceived as subjective transcendence still holds, but now there is a horizontal as well as a vertical dimension to transcendence. The "supreme insight concerning man's true greatness, his transcendence of earthly realities" needs revision.[40] Our true greatness lies not in being able to rocket ourselves away from the world but rather in opening ourselves more deeply to it. We get beyond ourselves in order to better attend to the rest of the world.

Epistemological humility in our understanding of God reinforces this. Self-transcendence for the sake of self-transcendence seems arbitrary and pointless, an empty mystery. It is incomplete if it merely distances us from the given and propels us into the unknown—if it is merely an individual exercise in relentless "why" questions. It is also incomplete if its social function is merely to insulate us from others, freedom-from without freedom-for. Self-transcendence needs to be used as a step toward respecting other selves, other beings, and other processes, rather than as a one-way ticket to the abyss. To speak ecologically, its completeness is in feeding value back into the system rather than taking value from it. It ought to go outward and downward after it goes inward and upward.

We developed our current understanding of human dignity to protect the person from both nature and culture. We fear reduction to physical or biological patterns, or to sociopolitical systems. In the process of overcoming such reductionism however, we have risked reducing nature and culture to us. We have tried to militate against that with regard to culture, seeking to build a social dimension into human personhood that is simultaneously morally challenging without being objectifying.[41] I think it is time to do the same with nonhuman nature, building its constitutive reality into our notion of human dignity complete with the moral challenges that that brings on, without simply reducing ourselves to the nonhuman in the process. Our social teachings insist that human dignity requires not only the protection of the individual but his or her ensconcement within a larger framework of historical-cultural-political meaning and obligation; does human dignity not also require that we understand and fit into our larger natural context? That we ensconce ourselves within the yet larger framework of life-projecting, eco-evolutionary nature from which we also derive meaning and obligation?

Moreover, as we have done with culture (which so often has been the underlying meaning of the term "world" when the relationship between Christianity, the church, and the world is really parsed out), we must ideally locate some soteriological significance to our ethically-based interrelation with nature, some sense that our moment of eco-evolutionary crisis today is of as much "vital concern to the kingdom" as the political and economic efforts we pursue in its name. We need our ethic to be "primary" in a theological as well as a moral sense: we need nature to have intrinsic soteriological as well as normative status.

There is something both irreducibly human and human-transcending about an environmental ethic. It calls us out of ourselves, yet in so doing it simultaneously appeals to our distinctive humanness: our capacity to value and act with respect for integrities that are not our own. It calls us to use our agency—that which qualitatively separates us from the nonhuman world—in order to rejoin ourselves, in some sense, to that nonhuman world. It calls us to use our knowledge of the wider world—a quality that we have often felt makes us superior to all other life-forms—to realize our smallness within it and its independence from us. In biblical language, it calls us to combine the God-like powers of Adam with the humility of Job, our sense of the world as our task with the vastly independent and awesome goodness of non-human creation.

SOME METHODOLOGICAL CONCERNS

The basic methodological direction that I think Catholicism ought to prefer in an environmental ethic is now evident. What follows will make it more explicit, summarizing the general approach, and contrasting it with other available options.

The key is respect for nature rather than love or reverence. As Marti Kheel writes, respect "is, in short, an invitation . . . literally to 'look again'."[42] I choose respect because it implies a receptivity on our part, a taking in, an attentiveness and an openness with regard to the world around us. These are crucial elements in appreciation as they are in understanding and successful instrumental use as well. Respect counters domination and aggression, but it also leaves room for transformation and use. One can use, transform, even kill, and show respect in some sense.

Reverence, as the foundation for an environmental ethic, seems to lead us too radically toward total passivity as well as to threaten an over-immanentization of God in nature. This threat is the danger of a "Cosmic Christ" type of approach, which makes God powerfully immanent in the creation, but understandably leaves out the ethical details of such a vision (beyond the rhetorical endorsement of the general eco-concern).[43] As in political issues, one can be paralyzed into the status quo by effectively identifying the deity with it (the Divine Right of Kings, for example). But I do not think this move is any more appropriate in our relations to the natural world than it is in the political arena. It verges on a monotheistic equivalent of animism with results that threaten to be paralytically conservative.

Love is a multifaceted term, with a long history of argument over its proper Christian meaning. There is a sense of love as relational that I think does not apply to our encounter with nature, and I am not sure whether radical self-sacrifice is appropriate behavior toward the nonhuman world. Still one can love nature in an other-centered sense as well as in an experiential sense (falling in love with a place, for example). I by no means exclude love (or reverence for that matter) as a category of human relationship vis-à-vis nature, but I do shy away from them as the foundation of an environmental ethic.[44] Perhaps they could be understood more as eco-counsels than eco-duties, or as states of especially rich eco-virtue rather than the minimum basic norm.

Our respect for nature is a valuational response to what nature really is. I do not mean this in any grandiose epistemological sense, but on a more commonsense level. Our valuation emerges from our perception and understanding of its makeup and functioning rather than because of attributes not generally perceivable to the human eye. We need not attribute spirits to animals and plants or conceive of intrinsic worth as some reified thing somewhere "inside" the animal (next to the liver perhaps) or locate nature's value in what it is projected to be like at some climactic, religious end-time. Theologically the task is to ratify and deepen our understanding of the goodness we find in creation as it is, not to add something "extra" to it.

Authors like Leopold and Rolston develop their norms in and through beautifully detailed descriptions of organisms, places, and ecosystems. Their ethic is therefore importantly science-based, though not reductively. It ultimately evolves out of valuationally sensitive, scientifically informed, nature experience. As Rolston explains it,

Evaluation is not scientific description; hence not ecology per se, but metaecology. No amount of research can verify that the right is the optimum biotic community. Yet ecological description generates this evaluation of nature . . . the description and evaluation to some extent arise together, and it is often difficult to say which is prior and which is subordinate.[45]

Such an ethic will therefore be subject to criticism based on empirical data as well as moral logic and valuational sensibilities. Our scientific perceptions of the world will impact, organically, our valuational understanding of it, both on the small scale (in terms of how we balance out competing values in particular instances) and on the large. For instance, should we find that natural history seems after all not to have any directionality whatsoever, then our fundamental option would have to be recast in different terms, or at the extreme, given up.

It is worth repeating that the use of science is not reductive but critical. Certainly part of the richness of our relationship to nature comes through imaginative wordplay using metaphor and simile; at a religious level nature cannot but be put into a larger symbolic context. Nor is any of this to say that there are no other ways to truly understand nature "as it really is" besides science. Our modern scientific worldview can be myopic. Certainly the human experience embedded in much traditional wisdom, religious or otherwise, often contains insight that we ignore at our peril. My point is not to cut these associations off altogether, but to tether them to our best scientific understanding of our world to date.

In terms of substantive moral content, our ethic centers itself at the level of the life-producing system of eco-evolutionary nature itself, of which we are a part. Thus, rather than ethically centering on individual organisms, we ground ourselves in the source of value-production and work outward to the products themselves. There are no organisms without species, no species without habitat, and no habitat without systemic health and dynamism.

The ethic starts by making a fundamental option for this state of affairs or, in different language, by making the goodness of fitting into this system a basic precept of the natural law. At this level we do not claim to solve all specific problems but to orient ourselves toward nature in a basically positive way. This foundational ethical orientation poses a direct challenge to our current one as we continue to move toward reducing the number of species on the planet by twenty percent over a period of a few decades. At present, we simply are not fitting into our environment.

Our ethic seeks to maintain, however, the qualitative distinction between the treatment of humans and nonhumans, though there is now a moral dimension to both. It looks to nonhuman nature for what it is and to humans for what we are and respects both accordingly.

There is thus a suspicion of methods that seem to slur the distinction either by reducing humans to the nonhuman world or by bringing nonhumans into our moral community *simpliciter.*

We seek then a scientifically informed, valuationally sensitive, weakly holistic ethic of respect for nature. There is not space to deal fairly with the myriad of other approaches currently being pursued; nevertheless it is worthwhile to pose some general contrasts with other approaches in order to clarify further the one I am suggesting.

Given the shape of our ethic, three more radical types of approaches are called into question: those that would drastically subsume the human species to the larger whole; those that would equate the human species with all others; and those that would project distinctively human moral categories and sensitivities onto nonhuman nature. Each will be commented on briefly and in turn.

The position I have earlier termed "strong holism" radically subsumes humanity to the larger natural system. For radical biocentrists, the good of the biotic community becomes the ultimate basis on which to judge right and wrong, with humans given no special consideration in that judgment.[46] For some deep ecologists, human selfhood becomes submerged into the larger system through an *identification* with the natural whole.[47] For advocates of a new cosmology a "primary allegiance" to the earth community is called for, reflecting the "primacy of nature" and a sense "of the human as a function of the earth."[48] Although these various approaches cannot simply be slurred together, their shared tendency toward strong holism creates a family resemblance among them.

Envisioning humans as merely one cog in the larger earth-organism, perhaps merely subordinate to the well-being of the planet as a whole, would certainly reverse our current direction if taken to heart. Granted there is no point in an environmental ethic that poses no challenge, even drastic challenges, to the current direction of our life on the planet.[49] But there is a danger in overstepping the level of theory and vision in order to address an admittedly drastic situation on the practical level. In the long-term, one wonders if such a vision contains the seeds of anticulture misanthropy, a basic blindness to the full wonder of who we are, and a threat to human dignity (one imagines eco-laws paralleling the coercive one-child policy in China, for example).

It must be said that a strongly holistic vision does not necessarily imply using humans simply as instruments for the health of the whole. The question of how to achieve the vision is to some extent separable from the vision itself. The authors cited thus far, for example, advocate and practice a consciousness-raising rather than coercive strategy, focusing on the conversion of minds and hearts. Be that as it may, there is also a tendency among them to leave the full ethical implications of their visions quietly unanalyzed in any systematic way (or to be blunt, facilely fudged).

These approaches also tend overly to aggrandize nonintervention at the expense of taking full account of the importance of our moral agency at this juncture of history. As Rolston argues, things may take care of themselves

> . . . in spontaneous natural systems when uninterrupted by human activities, but . . . if biological conservation is to succeed at all, one needs active environmental managers. . . . One needs studies of where the DDT is going . . . what the minimum thresholds of viable breeding populations are, what damage is done by exotic parasites and feral animals, how much the water table is falling.[50]

The extreme rejection of dominion that at times accompanies such views (and even more often, the views of certain ecofeminists) threatens to extinguish any sense of moral agency as well as obscure the radical facticity of our present power, which we can only control through self-conscious decisions. Even if we constrain or give up our power at this point, we are still yielding to an act of dominion. The reductive anthropocentrism often intertwined with dominion surely has to go; nature is not simply "for us," and claims such as "the earth and everything that is in it have been made specifically to be our home" must be rejected as incompatible with modern science and important scriptural strands, such as Job.[51] Still, the fact of holding nature in our hands cannot be ignored.

In that respect the "old" story seems hardly archaic; rather it seems to have come true with a vengeance, which is the only reason we are talking about this in the first place. Two key elements in the old story are that we have unique powers over nature and that what the planet ultimately looks like depends on how we use these powers. For this use we are accountable—to God and to each other—because nature is good. We are now at the climactic moment of irrevocable decision. Before seeking a completely new story, I think we need to finish this one. It is ethically and theologically imperative that we finish it well.

A second general approach, organismic egalitarianism, is avoided for two reasons.[52] First, it locates itself at the level of the individual rather than the system, which seems both axiologically and ecologically wrongheaded. Second, egalitarian approaches tend toward removing detail from our ethical analysis, making everything morally irrelevant so that we are all reduced to the same moral playing field. In our approach, as Ralston emphasizes, the task is to take in as much of reality as possible—to appreciate differences, not erase them.

Finally, there is concern that many of the approaches today project human moral categories and sensitivities on the nonhuman community in an inappropriate way. The implication is that nature somehow shares in the distinctively human way of being moral and therefore ought to be treated as we treat persons. The premise is not true, the conclusion not feasible. As John Passmore has argued:

> If men were ever to decide that they ought to treat plants, animals, landscapes precisely as if they were persons, if they were to think of them as forming with man a moral community in a strict sense, that would make it impossible to civilize the world—or, one might add, to act at all or even to continue living.[53]

The problem with extending rights-language to the nonhuman community (and here again I agree with Ralston) is precisely that such language seems to function most coherently within the human community itself. On the whole it is a moral tool for distinctively human purposes and with distinctively human prerequisites. The appeal to rights makes the individual inviolable in certain respects by the larger society—a task appropriate to transcendental subjectivity to be sure, but not necessarily appropriate, as a principle of treatment, to nonhuman nature (except in the case of higher animals perhaps). Moreover it can be argued (as the Catholic tradition does) that holding rights generally entails reciprocal responsibilities and duties, a reciprocality that nonhumans cannot share. Thus, rights tend to be interwoven with the human moral community of mutual responsibility and their extension into the nonhuman world cannot be carried too far without breaking down the concept.

Problematic in a similar way are notions such as extending a covenant to nature or seeing nature as an arena of mutuality and love. Here human categories seem misused, nature being morally elevated on the pretense of distinctly human forms of interaction rather than simply in response to how nature presents itself to us. Richard Gula, for example, states that "the moral community lives by *the same* covenantal principle which governs the working of the universe, namely, the principle of cooperative community." This "scientific and covenantal principle" is (and here he quotes Patricia Mische) that "love, cooperation, communion, is . . . what makes the universe work."[54] This statement is plainly false. The way in which nonhuman nature holds together and achieves order out of chaos is qualitatively different from the way in which human beings achieve order with each other and God. The attribution of love, cooperation, and communion to nonhuman nature is either a fideistic leap in spite of everything we know about the universe scientifically or a poetic projection (in which case it cannot really do the ethical work it purports to do). Interestingly, Gula concludes by asking us to ". . . develop those modes of cooperation which respect the functional integrity of the universe."[55] But we can do that without pretending that its functional integrity is the same as it is for the human community. We need not anthropomorphize nature, or make it more tender than it really is, to respect its life-creating and life-sustaining powers.

Finally, a word needs to be said about the concept of interdependence. For many, it is the category of choice for understanding our relationship to nature both descriptively and normatively. It is rooted in the ecological mind-set and it seems to move us past difficult issues of anthropo- versus biocentrism and the like. In the end, we and earth are in this drama together, and we should work out from that assumption.

I have argued that we must be careful not to make nature out to be human; we also have to be careful not to make humans out to be too natural in a self-applauding sort of way. The notion of interdependence threatens to do that, however.

We do have a relationship of interdependence with nature, but we must be careful how we understand it. Basically we are dependent on nature and nature is not dependent on us, except insofar as it needs us to redress the very destruction we have caused in the first place. In short, speaking ecologically, nonhuman nature would probably be better off without us, and much of the "power" we have over it is both a natural and ethical aberration that is primarily destructive. As Callicott says, our adaptive population in North America should be roughly twice that of bears.[56] So we should not play too fast and loose with the "inter" in interdependence as if nature is in principle as dependent on us as we are on it. We want to be careful about misrepresenting what nature can give to us (for example love and communion), but we must also be wary of what we say we can give to nature. If environmental ethics is successful, it will in large part be giving nature back to itself.

Our good and nature's good are intertwined in a very deep sense. But there is also a sense in which they are not intertwined and part of an adequate environmental ethic is to understand this divergence. Nature's transcendence *of* us must be felt and understood; interdependence by itself is thus not sufficient as a conceptual framework for an environmental ethic.

A FINAL WORD:
ENVIRONMENTAL ETHICS AND ESCHATOLOGY

As we intimated earlier, taking this direction in our ethic has implications for how we understand eschatology. In this approach we invest in nature as it is perceived now. Our task is to understand and defend our valuation of the nonhuman world we know, not one that we imagine. We do not defer our ethical affirmation to what nature will be like after the eschaton. But we cannot divorce ourselves from it either, lest our ethic become theologically secondary. The theological task is then, as it is in social and political ethics, to make eschatology work for this world, not against it. That nature matters eschatologically is functionally important for our task, but how it matters raises special problems for environmental ethics.

In social ethics there is a meaningful reciprocality between what we seek to achieve in society and the substantive vision of the kingdom in scripture. Thus, there is meaningful content to the eschatological vision: we seek to draw society toward the kingdom values of peace, justice, love, and equality. The substance of the eschatological vision of nature, however, offers no such meaningful reciprocality. In short, the vision seems to be one of noncompetitive, nonviolent domestication. But this vision is directly at odds with the mechanisms of the system as we know it and its products.

If the nature we really value is nature renewed at the end of time, and if that nature is portrayed as conflict free, then the nature we are really valuing has little to do with the nature of billions of years of eco-evolutionary development. Our issue is why we see this environment as good and why we want to stop ourselves from destroying it now. Grounding ourselves in the eschatological vision, however, does not draw out the values we already partially see in nature, but indicts the values we seek to respect.

I find this a serious problem in James Nash's *Loving Nature*, perhaps the most thorough Christian reflection on environmental ethics to date. In light of the violence in nature, Nash believes that "the classical theological propositions that the Creator and the creation are 'very good' are virtually indefensible . . . apart from an eschatological expectation."[57] As a result of ". . . the moral ambiguities of creation, we can experience only promising signs—not the full harmony—of the New Creation, the Peaceable Kingdom." He concludes: "Our moral responsibility, then, is to approximate the harmony of the New Creation to the fullest extent possible under the constricted conditions of the creation."[58] If that is so why is taming and domesticating nature not his primary norm rather than loving and respecting it in its present form?

Seeing present-day nature as good can, to be sure, cause theodicy problems. What do we make of the apparent waste, of the "red in tooth and claw" mechanism for both progress and stability? We can start by avoiding category mistakes: we do not morally evaluate natural inter-action as we do human interaction. I can hardly say to a vulture that its parasitic behavior is "reprehensible," as I would to my child should he act in a similar way. We are not out to judge nature morally (as if it were a moral agent) but to see if we can value it for what it is. Now we can say: I do not respect a system with so much carnage and waste in its mechanisms. Fair enough, but then we really need not have an envi-ronmental ethic but merely enlightened self-interest with regard to our surroundings, coupled with the hope that at some future time it will be a system we do respect.

It may also be possible, however, to see the evils as tributary to the goods—appreciating the mechanism in some sense (though not ideal-izing it).[59] Only if we can do something like this can we appreciate wild things and not automatically see domestication as an ideal. Lions lazing sleepily in a zoo, quietly taking the zookeepers daily meat-offer-ing, may seem "renewed" but in reality their brains have deteriorated. The lion that eats from my hand has lost the powerful and keen quali-ties that make it a lion, has lost its adaptive fitness and much of its maj-esty. The magnificence of a lion is intertwined with its need to hunt, as the grace of the antelope is intertwined with its need to escape. As Rolston argues, we cannot appreciate the products without appreciat-ing the system out of which they emerge.

The substantive vision of the end-time, insofar as it is the norm on which we base our actions, undercuts environmental ethics. This does not rule out anticipated renewal or a desire to have the same natural values be the product of nonviolent mechanisms. It does make the scriptural vision of the renewal problematic, even irrelevant, for our task. Perhaps it should be understood merely as a metaphorical projec-tion of human ideals (peace) on to nonhuman nature. I suggest that we preserve the hope that nonhuman nature is included in the end-time, but shy away from making our poetic anticipations of that vision nor-matively relevant for our action today. Perhaps we should simply say that grace will transform nature in a way continuous with, yet radi-cally different from, what it is now. How that can be and what that will look like, we do not know. But let us stress the continuity and work to enhance the good we find here rather than undercut our efforts to save the good on the basis of a future we see darkly at best.

This hope does not mean that we should crudely immanentize God's presence in nature; it does mean that we should work to see the good in nature. We must, in a profound theological sense, locate our-selves here, treating the earth as our promised land. We either do so or give up an environmental ethic in any primary sense.

NOTES

1. The institutional aspect of the church has already started this task. See for example John Paul II's reflections on ecological concern in *Sollicitudo rei socialis*. 1987. Nn. 26, 29, and 34; *The Ecological Crisis: A Common Responsibility*, World Day of Peace Message, January 1, 1990; and *Centesimus annus*. 1991. Nn. 31, 37–38, and 53. The most provocatively nonanthropocentric treatment occurs in the World Day of Peace message, though even this is pervaded with ambiguity. *Centesimus annus* seems decidedly anthropocentric. For a brief treatment of this, see my "John Paul II and Environmental Concern: Problems and Possibilities," *The Living Light* 28(1): 44–52. A stronger statement has been given by the U.S. Bishops in their pastoral statement *Renewing the Earth: An Invitation to Reflection and Action on the Environment in Light of Catholic Social Teaching*, 14 November 1991.

2. *A Sand County Almanac*, (New York: Ballantine Books, 1970), 239.

3. Ibid., 262.

4. *Man's Responsibility for Nature* (New York: Charles Scribner's Sons, 1974), 187.

5. The history can largely be traced in the journal *Environmental Ethics*, which began in 1979.

6. See, for example, Charles Hartshorne, "The Rights of the Subhuman World," *Environmental Ethics* 1. Spring 1979; Peter Miller, "Value as Richness." *Environmental Ethics* 4 (Summer 1982), 49–60.

7. See, for example, John Rodman, "Four Forms of Ecological Consciousness Reconsidered," in Donald Scherer and Thomas Attig, eds. *Ethics and the Environment* (Englewood Cliffs, NJ: Prentice Hall, Inc. 1983); and Paul Taylor, "The Ethics of Respect for Nature," *Environmental Ethics* 3 (November 1981).

8. See for example, J. Baird Callicott, "Animal Liberation: A Triangular Affair," in *Ethics and the Environment*: "The good of the biotic community is the ultimate measure of moral value, the rightness or wrongness of actions" (61). Further:

The biospheric perspective does not exempt *Homo sapiens* from moral evaluation in relation to the well-being of the community of nature taken as a whole. . . . The extent of misanthropy in modern environmentalism thus may be taken as a measure of the degree to which it is biocentric (65).

9. See Holmes Rolston III, *Philosophy Gone Wild: Essays in Environmental Ethics* (Buffalo, NY: Prometheus Books, 1986), and *Environmental Ethics: Duties to and Values in the Natural World* (Philadelphia: Temple University Press, 1988), for a representative of this approach. These include essays from the mid-seventies and after. I believe this is the richest, most thorough, and most methodologically sound attempt at an environmental ethic to date as well as generally amenable to Catholic appropriation. His influence on my thinking is clear throughout this paper—in some sense the task of the paper is to hook up Catholic moral theology with the general direction of his approach.

10. *Environmental Ethics*, 2.

11. From this point forward when I use "nature" I will mean nonhuman nature unless otherwise indicated by modifier or context.

12. The most nuanced treatment that I have found is by Rolston. See *Environmental Ethics*, Chapter 6.

13. As Callicott has argued:

It is possible that while things may only have value because we (or someone) values them, they may nonetheless be valued for themselves as well as for the contribution they might make to the realization of our (or someone's) interests (64).

14. Just as it is a fallacy to reduce altruism to self-centeredness because ultimately the person "desires" to be altruistic, so it is a fallacy to reduce intrinsic valuation to moral anthropocentrism simply because it is a human doing the valuing. In each case, there is an equivocation between describing the source of the action and the nature of the action in question.

15. Again I think Rolston generally does a good job of meeting this challenge—better than most environmental ethicists. For a provocative theological exploration of this challenge, see John Haught, "Religious and Cosmic Homelessness: Some Environmental Implications," in *Liberating Life: Contemporary Approaches to Ecological Theology*, ed. Charles Birch, William Eakin, and Jay B. McDaniel (Maryknoll, NY: Orbis, 1980). "Evolutionary thinking has made it possible for us . . . to locate our own creative subjectivity within the context of a more comprehensive one, that of the universe itself" (171). We and the universe share in a "cosmic adventure," both of us sharing in an "inherent exploratory restlessness" (173). We care for the world not because we want to preserve the monotonous status quo, but because we see it as a process, a story, of adventurous emergence of which both our appreciation and transformation of it are a part.

I am in basic agreement with this approach though I worry that in the end notions of cosmic adventure coupled with a heavy emphasis on mystery lead just as easily to radical transformation of the world as to appreciative harmony with it. For instance, why not view a catastrophic extinction as just another turn into the unknown of cosmic adventure? We are here, after all, in part because the dinosaurs are not.

16. I owe this point to Arthur Ekirch, *Man and Nature in America* (Lincoln: University of Nebraska Press, 1973), 23.

17. Our necessarily conflictual relationship to nature poses a problem for the kind of consistency sought for by Kantians. We simply cannot treat all of nature in the same way, much less its various components. Some will be sacrificed, others transformed, others preserved. Perhaps a Kantian approach to environmental ethics could overcome this problem by making respect for nature an imperfect duty.

18. See, for example, Linda Graber, *Wilderness as Sacred Space* (Washington, DC: The Association of American Geographers, 1976).

19. Note the astounding change in lifestyle in the United States over the last one hundred years. We have shifted from a majority living in rural areas to fewer than five percent.

20. It is illuminating here to note the development of many environmental ethicists beyond radically preservationist attitudes. For example, see Baird Callicott's insistence on an integrated approach in Genesis, and John Muir's *Covenant for a New Creation: Ethics, Religion, and Public Policy*, ed. Carol Robb and Carl Casebolt (Maryknoll, NY: Orbis, 1991).

21. The modern nature experience is made possible precisely because of scientific management and planning of recreation areas, modern transportation, modern camping equipment, an economy that creates a mobile middle-class, among other things.

22. Rolston, *Environmental Ethics*, 43.

23. See his *The Travail of Nature* (Philadelphia: Fortress Press, 1985), 9–10.

24. Richard Gula, *Reason Informed by Faith: Foundations of Catholic Morality* (Mahweh, NY: Paulist Press, 1989), 80.

25. Rolston, *Environmental Ethics*, 24–25.

26. For an account of this, see Rolston, *Environmental Ethics*, 154–158. "Species packing" is a term he takes from R. H. Whittaker.

27. Ibid., 10.

28. Ibid., 43.

29. See Bertrand Russell, "A Free Man's Worship," in *Why I am not a Christian* (New York: Simon and Schuster, Inc., 1957).

30. *Summa theologiae*, I.II.94.a2.

31. For a sampling of modern scholarship on Thomas and the natural law, see *Readings in Moral Theology 7: Natural Law and Theology*. ed. Charles E. Curran and Richard A. McCormick (Mahwah, NY: Paulist Press, 1991).

32. Timothy O'Connell, *Principles for a Catholic Morality*. Rev. ed. (San Francisco: Harper and Row, 1990), 172 (emphasis mine). Even Gula, who is much more environmentally sensitive and even provocative in his approach than O'Connell, writes: "The great moral implication of the person as subject is that no one may ever use a human person as an object or as a means to an end the way we do other things in the world" (68). The key to human morality lies in an objectifying contrast to the nonhuman world.

33. David Hollenbach, *Claims in Conflict: Retrieving and Renewing the Catholic Human Rights Tradition* (New York: Paulist Press, 1979), 89 (emphasis mine).

34. Ibid., 73.

35. N. 39.

36. This is not true for the deep ecologists who focus quite heavily on the transformation of consciousness and experience in nature. Their vision of what it means to be human in nature is, however, different from ours.

37. Kenneth Goodpaster, "On Being Morally Considerable," in Scherer and Attig, *Ethics and the Environment*.

38. "Storied achievement" is Rolston's way of articulating the salient value of life at the level of the species.

39. *A Sand County Almanac*, 117.

40. John Paul II, *Centesimus annus*, n. 13.

41. See, for example, David Hollenbach's efforts in *Claims in Conflict*.

42. Marti Kheel, "Ecofeminism and Deep Ecology: Reflections on Identity and Difference," in *Covenant for a New Creation*, p. 160.

43. See, for example, Matthew Fox, *The Coming of the Cosmic Christ* (San Francisco: Harper and Row, 1988).

44. For a strong argument in favor of love as a foundational category in a Christian approach to nature, see Jim Nash's *Loving Nature: Ecological Integrity and Christian Responsibility* (Nashville, TN: Abingdon Press, 1991), especially 93–161. In brief outline the argument runs: God loves the world; we are in the image of God; to be in the image of God is to love what God loves. Moreover, Christ is the perfection of this image and thus a paradigm of dominion. And that paradigm is nurturing and serving love.

My instincts are to say, however, that we do not so much serve nature as respect it, nurture it as let it take its own course. God loves nature as God's own creation, but nature is not our creation. The way in which God is connected to it is different from the way we are, or can be, connected to it. This topic needs more discussion.

45. Rolston, "Is there an Ecological Ethic?" in *Philosophy Gone Wild*, 19.

46. For example, see J. Baird Callicott, *Covenant for a New Creation*.

47. For a critical analysis of this theme in deep ecologists, see Marti Kheel's critique in "Ecofeminism and Deep Ecology."

48. Thomas Berry, *The Dream of the Earth* (San Francisco: Sierra Club Books, 1988), 43, 48; and "The Spirituality of the Earth," in *Liberating Life*, 153.

49. For myself, I believe the drastic challenges need to come not in assaults on individual interests but in the rethinking of national sovereignty.

50. "Science-based Versus Traditional Ethics," in *Ethics of Environment and Development*. ed. J. Ronald Engel, and Joan Gibb Engel, (Tucson, AZ: University of Arizona Press, 1990), 68–69.

51. I here quote Charles Murphy, *At Home on Earth: Foundations for a Catholic Ethic of the Environment* (New York: Crossroad, 1989), 6.

52. For a rigorous defense, see Paul Taylor, *Respect for Nature: A Theory of Environmental Ethics* (Princeton: Princeton University Press, 1986).

53. *Man's Responsibility for Nature*, 126.

54. *Reason Informed by Faith*, 94.

55. Ibid., 95.

56. J. Baird Callicott, "Animal Liberation," 65.

57. *Loving Nature*, 99.

58. Ibid., 132–133.

59. Rolston pursues this line of thought at some length. See, for example, *Environmental Ethics*, 22–23, 42–43, 162–67, 218–22.

Nature's God and the God of Love

DREW CHRISTIANSEN

Our first national monument, the Pinnacles, receives its name from several chimney like structures, the natural weather-carved remains of half a volcano that migrated north along the San Andreas Fault millions of years ago. The other half of the peak lies more than two hundred miles south on the other side of the fault.

Some years ago, my friends and I took an early winter camping trip to this monument. It was my first desert camping trip and I was astonished by many things. From one peak we saw what appeared to be a mountain only recently split, just as Pinnacles had been aeons before, by a geologic fault.

We clambered through talus caves, narrow canyons roofed in by boulders. Later we explored parklike box canyons with flowing springs, lacy digger pines, and buckeyes in fruit.

But as we came to the top of our last climb over a ridge called the Balconies we came on the most astonishing sight of all: a group of handicapped people in the company of young volunteers were climbing the mountain; they traveled in self-powered wheelchairs, on crutches, or limped along with the support of their friends.

That night, as I sat under the desert sky amazed at the plentitude of the heavens and all I had seen that day, Immanuel Kant's dictum came to mind. He said that for him there were two things that inspired genuine awe: "the starry sky above and the moral law within."

Of all the wonderful things we had seen that day, the most wonderful by far was the expedition on the Balconies—women and men on crutches and in wheelchairs exploring Pinnacles in the company with their friends.

The moral I would like to draw from my Pinnacles encounter is this: Christianity, and Catholicism in particular, have a significant contribution to make to ecological theology and ethics. The contribution of biblical religion needs to be explored dialectically to use Dan Cowdin's phrase: "in critical correlation" with our ever-growing knowledge of God's action in creation.

Sharing the Pinnacles hike with handicapped and able-bodied hikers was for me an event that was only possible because the ideal of Christian love for the weak and vulnerable had somehow really penetrated a culture. It was not the outcome of any lesson that we can find in nature.[1]

With this experience as background, I make three points in response to Dan Cowdin's rich and provocative paper. First, beginning with theological method, I propose that natural revelation by itself is an inadequate base on which to build a Christian environmental theology. Therefore, both historic revelation and Christian moral experience are necessary elements in a Christian response to the environmental crisis.

Second, drawing from the tradition of moral theology, I propose that the method of analogy and the principles of Catholic social teaching offer us helpful ways to think about issues of environmental justice.

And, third, I dissent from Dan Cowdin's proposal for "a fundamental option for nature." Instead I propose that Richard Niebuhr's "ethics of responsibility" offers a more coherent approach to environmental theology—one that combines elements of creation theology with elements of historic revelation in Christ.

METHOD: NATURE'S GOD AND THE GOD OF LOVE

One of the traditional themes of Catholic theology in contrast to Reformation theology is the notion that God is revealed in nature. For most of this century, Karl Barth and other Neoorthodox theologians like Paul Tillich and Reinhold Niebuhr have vigorously challenged the notion of "natural theology." In recent years, some younger Roman Catholic theologians, accepting the biblicist and existential assumptions of contemporary Protestantism, turned their backs on natural theology, but this rejection never became a consensus position in either systematic theology or ethics. In one form or another, natural-law styles of thinking have remained the currency of debate.

Creation theology has generated two kinds of misconception: first, ignorance about the strength of natural revelation in the Catholic tradition; and second, a practical rejection of historic revelation (the Bible and tradition) as a pertinent source for environmental theology. It is to the relevance of historic Christian revelation for environmental ethics that I would like to draw our attention.

The Ambiguity of Cosmic Revelation

A few weeks ago in Washington, D.C., the nature writer and paleontologist, Stephen Jay Gould, addressed a Jewish convocation on the issue of species extinction. In his conclusion, Gould admitted a limit that environmental theologians need to take seriously in their efforts to draw on cosmology as a basis for ethics.

For Gould, the passage of life on earth as we know it is a given. In the paleontologists' time scale, species evolve and disappear, leaving only fossilized skeletons behind. As a scientist, Gould told the audience, he could not offer them a reason to preserve the earth as it is. "There was life on earth before humans appeared," he said, "and I must assume there will be life even when humans pass from the scene."

Cosmology does not lead to faith or to an ethics of care for the earth. Jim Gustafson, the dean of Christian ethicists in the United States, anticipated current debates some ten years ago in his *Ethics from a Theocentric Perspective*.[2] Gustafson attempted to take the findings of science very seriously, but while his reliance on the physical sciences allowed him to affirm evidence of a divine ordering in nature, it did not help him to affirm that God is good. In its oscillation between creation and destruction, between beauty and terror, the cosmos does not offer any firm instruction about care for others. The book of nature yields at best an ambiguous message.

The ambiguity of natural revelation, especially with respect to ethics, explains why Christian tradition paired the book of nature with the book of God's acts. For it is in the biblical narratives, and more generally in the experience of the Jewish and Christian communities, that the ultimate goodness of creation is affirmed. Only the believing community's experience of God's constant love through time moves us out of the impasse brought about by the ambiguities of earth and cosmos.

In particular it is by encountering the self-giving love of Christ and his teachings on the law of love that we develop the depths of care from which emerges the sustained and sensitive commitment necessary to preserve creation.

By popular acclaim and papal declaration, Francis of Assisi has been named patron of the environment. As we develop an environmental theology, we would do well to remember that Francis learned his special love for creatures only after he had been engaged for many years in the struggle to care for "God's little ones," the lepers. His imitation of Christ grew from care for the marginal and despised to intimacy with birds and wolves.[3] A properly Christian eco-theology must, I think, begin with what Dante called "the love that moves the stars." That the Unmoved Mover (Gustafson's Divine Orderer) is the God of love is a truth we know through historic revelation.

"Have this Mind in You . . . "

Saint Francis's religious and moral development holds another lesson for the development of a Christian theology of the environment;

namely, eco-theology must be informed by Christian moral experience, in particular, the christoform (cruciform) experience of death and resurrection that lies at the center of the faith that was lived and celebrated by Francis and Gerard Manley Hopkins, among others.

Christian moral experience is, like the biblical witness and Christian tradition, a necessary component in eco-theology. As Michael Buckley points out in his *At the Origins of Modern Atheism*,[4] a very heavy emphasis on natural philosophy (science) in the theology of the seventeenth and eighteenth centuries preceded the rise of modern atheism. Theologians ceased to draw on the explicitly religious dimensions of life—on prayer, the evidence of holy lives, the reading of scripture—for their argument. As a result, when their cosmology was found wanting, so were their theological arguments. The consequence was a loss of faith, but faith had already been displaced by the alleged certitudes of contemporary science.

The return to cosmology in contemporary theology must avoid repeating the mistakes of the Enlightenment. To do so, however, requires a dialectical integration of science and cosmology with scripture, tradition, and the experience of the Christian life.

The people of faith who suffer in the defense of the environment, and the poor who understand the relation between justice and the integrity of creation are witnesses to the relevance of traditional Christian moral experience to current environmental struggles. The path to the peaceable kingdom in which the lion shall lie down with the lamb always entails *kenosis*.

CHRISTIAN LOVE AND LOVE OF NATURE

So far I have argued that the God of love must play a central role in the construction of a Catholic environmental theology. Now I suggest that the law of love must also play a role in our relation to nature.

Analogy

Professor Cowdin has expressed some reservations about using a "love ethic" in relation to the natural world. I have in the past shared those reservations, but in recent months I have been reconsidering that position.

One factor that has contributed to my rethinking has been the appearance of James Nash's book, *Loving Nature: Ecological Integrity and Christian Responsibility*.[5] Nash takes on the challenge of relating environmental concerns to the heart of the Christian ethical tradition, "the love command," and does so convincingly in my judgment, but even his work could be strengthened by use of the scholastic concept of analogy. We know God's love primarily through love for humanity, but we can still speak meaningfully of "the love that moves the stars." Accordingly we can also speak in a meaningful way about a human love of nature.

Interestingly Nash uses the traditional Catholic understanding of Christian love as communion to develop the notion of the love of nature. "Communion" is a broad concept, especially if we use it as Thomas Aquinas did to embrace the divine-human encounter (e.g. the Eucharist), human friendship, nature mysticism, affection for pets, and care for the environment. What is missing in Nash's writing, however, is the qualification that these relations must be understood analogously, as the Dominican Thomas Gilby explained nearly forty years ago in his *Between Community and Society: A Philosophy and Theology of the State*.[6] Gilby's exposition of Thomistic political philosophy took communion as its central metaphor and at the same time made love a cosmological principle.

Autarchy and Koinonia

Another way in which Christian love relates to environmental ethics concerns environmental or green economics. The classic patristic doctrine of property, which was reaffirmed by the Second Vatican Council, holds that there are two goals for material possessions: sufficiency, in Greek *autarchia*, the provision of a decent life for each person; and sharing, in Greek *koinonia*, providing for those in need.[7]

Given the ecological limits of growth, these twin norms are all the more appropriate; they set limits to accumulation through a standard of sufficiency and promote the sharing of resources with the people of developing nations. If sustainable development means limiting economic growth, then sharing resources with the world's poor is necessary as Pope John Paul II said in his Lenten message earlier this year. Indeed, this necessity has been a constant of papal teaching on the environment. If there is a Christian contribution to be made to the environmental movement, it is above all to make the link between justice and the environment and to bridge the gap that divides the affluent North from the impoverished South.

ECOLOGICAL RESPONSIBILITY

Finally, my one exception to Dan Cowdin's paper is his proposal that what we need is "a fundamental option" for nature. My objection is essentially a theological one; namely, the fundamental option refers to what Paul Tillich called our ultimate concern. From a theological perspective, the object of such concern can only be the mystery of God. If one were to embrace a fundamental option for nature as some environmentalists and creation theologians propose, one would no longer be doing Christian theology. Cowdin alternately proposes that respect for nature ought to be defined as a principle of the natural law, though even here I would quibble. Respect for nature has to be a secondary, not a primary, principle of the natural law. It is not on a par with "Do good, avoid evil."

If we are looking for a theological framework in which to set an environmental ethic that takes into account the cosmological, personal, and divine, I propose that we consider H. Richard Niebuhr's responsibility ethic.[8] It looks at "wholes" in the way environmentalists like H. Holmes Ralston propose. The responsibility ethic also keeps alive the notion that one must respond to various dimensions of reality at the same time; one cannot subsume everything into a one dimensional model even if that model is ecological. And lastly, this ethic holds that Christ is the ultimate model of response and responsibility, thereby continuing to integrate Christian tradition and experience into a dynamic ethic.

SUMMARY

New developments in cosmology have offered us important insights for the elaboration of an environmental ethics. But cosmology also needs to be integrated dialectically with historical revelation in the form of biblical narrative and Christian moral experience. Of continuing relevance for a Christian environmental ethic are the love command, the method of analogy, the principles of autarchy and sharing, and a systematic ethics of responsibility.

NOTES

1. James Gustafson, *Ethics from a Theocentric Perspective* (Chicago: University of Chicago Press, 1981).

2. Leonardo Boff, *Saint Francis: A Model for Human Liberation* (New York: Crossroad Publishing, 1984).

3. William Buckley, *At the Origins of Modern Atheism* (New Haven, CT: Yale University Press, 1987).

4. James Nash, *Loving Nature: Ecological Integrity and Christian Responsibility* (Washington, DC: The Churches' Center for Theology and Public Policy, 1991).

5. Thomas Gilby, *Between Community and Society: A Philosophy and Theology of the State* (New York: Longmans, Green, 1955).

6. Charles Avila, *Ownership: Early Christian Teaching* (Maryknoll, NY: Orbis Books, 1983).

7. H. Richard Niebuhr, *The Responsible Self: An Essay in Christian Moral Philosophy* (New York: Harper and Row, 1963).

8. H. Holmes Ralston III, *Environmental Ethics: Duties to and Values in the Natural World* (Philadelphia: Temple University Press, 1989).